Other Books by Tony Seton

The Flight of KAL 007
The Bright Wise Solution
13 Days of Fear
Silent Alarm
Deki-san
Equinox
Mokki's Peak
No Soap, Radio
Paradise Pond
Selected Writings
The Autobiography of John Dough, Gigolo
Silver Lining
The Omega Crystal/New Moves
Truth Be Told
Mayhem
Jennifer
The Francie LeVillard Mysteries- Volumes I- X
Just Imagine
Trinidad Head
Musings on Sherlock Holmes
The Brink
Dead as a Doorbell
The Quality Interview / Getting it Right
   on Both Sides of the Mic
From Terror to Triumph /
   The Herma Smith Curtis Story
Don't Mess with the Press / How to Write,
   Produce, and Report Quality Television News
Right Car, Right Price

Is There a Why?

Is There a Why?

By Tony Seton

Carmel, California

April 2019

This book was written at different times in my life, but every word, expression, and thought in this book is true in fact and meaning as best as I can recall and report. All that is in these pages is offered not to persuade but to inform about one person's perspective.

Is There a Why?

ISBN-978-0-9989605-9-3

ISBN-10: 0-9989605-9-4

Printed in the United States

Author's Note

There is no Owner's Manual to being human. Most of us receive some basic instructions from our parents and siblings, and then school is supposed to give us a framework for guiding and managing our participation as functioning – and presumably productive – members of the community.

But technology and evolution have brought quantum changes that this process of societalization has failed to match. The schism between society's version of The Meaning of Life and the reality that confronts us has widened, creating such separate – sometimes disparate – descriptions as to rupture a critical adhesive between the individual and the society.

Society does not seem to be holding up, according to the general public perception, and that has caused great concern over the past few decades, concern which is now spiraling into fear that the very social fabric is tearing apart. Eight out of ten Americans are very or somewhat concerned about our democracy.

Is There a Why?

One might say that the good news is that we feel unsafe in our own neighborhoods, we believe our federal government is in the hands of incompetents, bureaucrats, and crooks, and we are seeing our institutions collapsing into failure. The bad news is that none of our political leaders is publicly recognizing the situation, let alone proposing solutions.

But what if there are no *solutions*?

What if our society can't be safe the way it is structured? What if we need a whole new kind of governance? And what if the age-old institutions cannot and will not meet our needs?

Then we don't actually want solutions but instead need a different perspective on what's happening to us.

What's happening in our society today, playing out in dramatic and upsetting headlines, is symptomatic of a much larger situation. Like a noise you find annoying, you try to block it out; then you cover your ears. But it's the whistle of an approaching train, which, by growing louder and annoying you to the point that you look up and get out of the way, saves your life. How do you feel about that annoying sound now?

What if the shredding of the safety net, the sale of the environment to campaign contributors, and the widespread violence among our youth are not really the problems, but rather are warnings? Symptoms of a widespread social dis-ease that will be unresolvable until we understand what is really going on in our lives.

I think that a different perspective, while overtly at odds with many aspects of the *official* view, can explain what's going on; that this perspective encompasses more of the circumstances which are ignored by society's explanation; and that it is ultimately more positive.

This perspective is neither new nor very complicated. In fact, many people have been writing about different aspects of this shifting of perspectives, and many millions of people have been buying their books, which suggests a certain resonance.

I lay out my description knowing that some of what I say is new and much has been said before. This isn't about ownership of ideas, as will be obvious in later pages. It is about putting into words a personal library of thoughts – old and new – that have been assimilated, manipulated, and is now being disseminated.

Originally I was going to call this book *A Philosophy of One* as there is no intention to attract or convert anyone to an ism. There is no wagon to hitch to. My expectation is that certain ideas or turns of phrases will find a connection with some people and will spark a useful synapse; which is what any writing should be about.

I would prefer not to speak in the first person, at risk of seeming egotistical, but all that is recounted here is from my own experience. I thought of trying to fashion a fictional story around the ideas herein, but maybe another time.

Also, I use masculine pronouns where generic rather than he-she and him-her, because I'm a he, but mostly so as not to waste paper and ink.

Anyway, as you will see, it is not important who I am or where I've been. Nor is it important that you believe everything that you read, although everything I recount is clear in my mind and accurate to my understanding. If you should find yourself questioning the veracity of some point, or feel yourself getting annoyed over something, stop a minute for a minute and remember that you're not being asked to buy, or even agree with, anything.

I'm telling what I know because I believe that a significant number of other people are experiencing similar thoughts and feelings. This recounting may help them to feel less alone, make connections in their own mind, and keep going on their own, personal exploration.

*   *   *   *   *

Is There a Why?

I wrote this book in 1996, 23 years ago, when I was living in "Marvy" Marin County. A month ago, I had started to write a book on consciousness. I searched my e-files for a short bit I remembered but didn't know where it was. I found it...in this book that I had forgotten about. I started to read it. Hmm. A lotta good stuff in here. Maybe I'll borrow it for the new book. I kept reading. This is very interesting; and I like the writing. I read it through.

Okay, I decided, the new book is considerably different. Yes, there is some overlap, but I should publish this book on its own.

So I have read it through, caught some the typos, clarified some dense thoughts, and updated some – but not all – of the time-related references. For instance, we were in serious trouble two decades ago. There have been some interesting changes in our lives; e.g., the internet, smartphones, the Tea Party, the Kardashians. And the socio-political situation seems to have gotten a lot worse. But, interestingly, the solutions preferred herein haven't changed. Thank you for getting this far. I hope you find useful ideas that might help you to chart a healthy and productive course.

Tony Seton
Carmel, California

Is There a Why?

Prologue

It is a question that seems to have escaped most of us, consumed as we are in and by our daily lives. Whaddya mean, Is There a Why?

Okay, why are you here? What is the purpose of your life? What will you have accomplished when it's time to shuffle off of this mortal coil? What will be your legacy, in fact and in memory?

And if you don't care about those questions – Hey, you have kids to put through college at $250,000 a pop – what is your true motivation in this life? What expectations do you have of yourself? Who's keeping you in line? Were you simply created by your parents, and in a number of years, it will just be dust to dust?

For some people, this may be enough. That was pretty much my view for the first half of my life. Brought up as I was by a semi-Freudian psychoanalyst father and a pseudo-Calvinist mother/writer who, at her death, was called "the Jane Austen of the Twentieth Century," my life was described this way: You're born, you die, you moulder in the grave, and in between you work hard and live an ethical life.

Not complicated, and mostly not difficult, especially since my parents led a thoughtful and proper life; (how appropriate that my mother's maiden name was Propper). My four younger sisters and I were very well behaved, and still are. So are my sisters' children.

There was love and respect in our home. We were never in need or even really in want. And what we didn't have – specifically, any sense of a spiritual component in life – we didn't miss. My mother's parents weren't church-goers. My father's parent were Jewish but religion was not a significant part of his growing up. In fact, his surname was Solomon but he and his brother changed it to Seton in 1943, when he was around 20, because of the widespread anti-Semitism.

(Sidebar: I learned this by a curious accident. I was on a Circle Line boat going around Manhattan with my aunt when I was 13. As we cruised by the Wall Street end of the island, the spieler noted that this was where Mother Elizabeth Seton practiced her good works with the poor. I asked my aunt if we were related. Surprised, she asked if I didn't know that my father and uncle had changed their name.

When I asked my father about this, he was annoyed that I had found out. Maybe he felt guilty about what they had done. Anyway, while I never was a deist or had an affiliation with any religion, I considered myself a member of The Tribe if people were espousing anti-Semitism.)

While my parents allowed, indeed encouraged, all of us children to attend any and all churches we might want, we all seemed to find better things to do on Sunday mornings.

(My youngest sister went to church for a while, but it never got serious. This was a person who at age six referred to the statue of Mary in the familiar lawn sculpture-pose under the arch as *virgin on a half-shell*.)

When I was her age, I had gone to Monday school briefly because I liked the orange drink they served, but I quit when the seasons changed and they started using a gas heater which gave off an odor I didn't like. Not a deep religious conviction.

My next religious encounter was at age ten, when my best friend, Bobby Prouser, was taken out of Saturday morning bowling league to study for his Bar Mitzvah. Neither of us saw much value in the choice.

Five years later, I was dispatched to prep school where church attendance of some denomination was mandatory. I signed up for Jew Cong (Jewish Congregation) because it was a ten-minute service on Friday night and I could have my Sundays free.

I grew up well and fast without god and *god-bothering-boxes*, as was our *haut* reference to churches. Raised as I was with a strong ethical base and an interest in leading a productive life, there didn't really seem to be anything missing. I thought that people who went to church basically did so out of habit or to palliate a family member.

I went to church a number of times myself – got married twice in them – but I never heard anything that even came close to talking-to me. This is not to say that there aren't some stimulating sermons now and again, and God-bless for that, but for the most part, what I heard felt like an overly-aggressive if droning sales pitch with a strong product-tampering warning.

And it was always about one god, the one with the long white hair and beard, who wore long white robes, and who dispensed remarkably painful lessons according to the Judaeo-Christian tradition of seemingly mindless purpose conjoined with blind faith. I simply couldn't buy the notion of a supreme being what with all the world's tragedies, and "He works in mysterious ways" wasn't an adequate explanation.

Religion to me looked a lot like the corresponding priests of science standing at a podium in their own long white lab coats with their hands behind their back, peering over their bottle-thick glasses lens, shaking their heads, saying "We don't know."

And they were right.

I spent my twenties (the Seventies) primarily in New York, working in television news. I was successful in my pursuits, which I enjoyed tremendously, and by age thirty had already been a network television news producer at ABC for several years. I had covered the Watergate trial and Senate hearings, six elections, five space shots; I had produced Barbara Walters' news interviews, met presidents and prime ministers, and won some national awards as producer of the business/economics coverage.

And after ten years, I was bored. News was a great place to be if you wanted things to change all the time. But curiously, with all that was happening in the world, the news industry, for that is what it had become, had lost its appeal.

Part of it was the politics of ABC and where the industry was headed. Years later former colleagues would say that I had gotten out at just the right time. All three networks had started going after the sizzle at the expense of the steak. A lot of other viewers got turned off, too. Network news viewership was at 85% of the television audience when I left in 1980, and today is maybe around 30%. Of course, there are many more choices of what to watch on *the idiot box* with satellite, cable, and streaming, and other places to watch entertainment, as well as other venues to get their news. Just saying, it ain't what it used to be.

My prescience aside, I decided to move to the San Francisco area, get married, and settle down. In October of 1980, I arranged for a company transfer to the ABC-owned station, KGO, and I moved from the concrete canyons of Manhattan to the redwood canyons of Mill Valley.

I thought that I pretty much had my life under control.

Two months later I was fired from KGO; the following spring, my marriage of 4½ months crashed and burned. And despite my significant communications credentials, I couldn't find anyone who even wanted to interview me for a corporate or agency PR position. I had put all of my savings into the purchase of the house, and I was out of money. So much for control.

*   *   *   *   *

It was during that first year in Mill Valley that I started meeting people who would suggest books, seminars, and other people, all of which/who wound up comprising an initiatory personal curriculum of spiritual education. It was a process that is clearer, of course, in retrospect; at the time it looked as disconnected as I felt. Not only were these people new to my life, but so was a lot of their thinking. This was not only the West Coast, and California, but also Marin Country.

I had made the decision to move to California after my first trip to the Bay Area in December of 1978. I remember riding in from the airport, over Portrero Hill, seeing San Francisco for the first time at night. And then the next morning, in the confirming light of day, I wondered why everyone didn't want to live here. This discovery startled me, since I had always viewed California through East Coast glasses: weird, self-indulgent, and frou-frou.

In fact, the reason for my trip to San Francisco was to advance a Barbara Walters' news story on how crazy was this San Francisco Bay Area; where they had assassinated the mayor and a supervisor, and from where the victims of the Jonestown tragedy had migrated. While there, I pre-interviewed Reg Murphy, then editor of the *San Francisco Examiner*, who said something to the effect that,

Of all the people who approach the line of insanity, 95% turn back. Of the five percent who don't, a disproportionate number come to California – something about

*manifest destiny, perhaps – and of that group, a dispro-
portionate number finds themselves in San Francisco, at
the end of a rocky peninsula, where "everything goes."
And if you still can't make it, well, then you're in serious trouble.*

As I discovered after I moved to Mill Valley two
years later, in this kind of *free* environment, there
are all sorts of confused and desperate people, and
many people ready to *help* them. Esalen, a birth-
place of the New Age, was just four hours down
the road in Big Sur, and there were limitless numbers of workshops and therapists available for
those who were searching, and who had the resources to spend on that search.

In all fairness, there are a lot of people who are
truly and diligently searching. And making some
important discoveries. But there are a lot of people
who are spending a lot of time just looking, trying
out one system after another without making a
serious attempt to grow or to change. Some people
become workshop junkies, and they never run out
of new fixes to explore.

In my first year, I encountered an array of truly
wonderful people and ideas; I also found the opportunity, and need, to develop new filtering pro-
cedures. And, for the first time in my life, I looked
into the non-scientific realm: I went to an astrologer, a psychic, and a palmist.

Is There a Why?

Chortle all you like; it's not a pretty sight doing the stereotype shuffle, eschewing the worldly sophistication of New York City, and engaging a whole new lexicon of precepts and notions which are not only in direct conflict with scientific reasoning – itself a 300-year religion – but that also look kind of kooky. Rational thought versus howling at the full moon on Mt. Tamalpais.

But when you're in the middle of a process, in a transition from what you *knew* to brand new, taking a flyer on what may seem weird but at least isn't harmful, it doesn't look as ridiculous from the inside as it does, often, from the outside. What is history, after all, but a chronicle of replaced belief systems.

Truth be told, these three *non-scientists* – the astrologer, psychic, and palmist – introduced to me by different friends, all got my attention by telling me things about my personal life that neither they nor the connecting people knew about me.

All three also told me in 1981 that I would help to change the world through communications.

I've always thought highly of my own communications skills, and wasn't alone in that opinion. I have a nose for news and know how to fit pictures and words together to report a story clearly. Changing the world seemed a bit high-minded, but

I certainly believed that the world needed some serious corrections, and if I could help – be part of the effort – why sure I'd be there.

At the same time, I was being given books that began to reveal to me whole areas of thinking that hadn't been part of my East Coast purview. I had never thought about spirituality; I thought it and organized religion were the same thing and I didn't think much of the latter. I appreciated integrity, perhaps more than the next guy, and I knew quality when I saw it. My view was, allowing for the odd coincidence and life was pretty much life.

Some of the new ideas to which I was exposed had both justification and appeal. For instance, this fellow Carl Jung said some interesting things about a collective unconscious, archetypes, mythology, and synchronicity. Not having taken psych101 – hey, my father was a shrink – this stuff was new to me. I never actually read Jung, but I read around him, in books by people who had.

When I first mentioned Jung in my family home, in front of my father, I didn't know that Freud and Jung were no longer sharing a tent, and the subject was summarily dismissed with that impatient certainty of disappointed silence that my father had exercised over the years when one of his children demonstrated a case of mis-aligned thoughts.

Along with Jung came some exposure to Eastern religions, and I found myself attracted to some of the Taoist ideas. Not as a convert, but as an intellectual. The simple practices, the personal responsibility, and the core desire for integrity and justice. *The Tao of Psychology* and *The Tao of Pooh* both got my attention, as did pieces of books by people like Robert Bly writing about revivified maleness.

Most significant to me was the work of Robert A. Johnson, especially *She*, a 70-page book first written in the early Seventies and re-issued a number of times since. It is a discussion of the feminine psychology using the myth of Aphrodite and Psyche. I've read it a number of times, sometimes as a litmus test for a possible paramour.

I consider *She* to be one of the most important books I've ever read. It illuminated mythic behavior patterns that are apparent in daily life, and in myself. What was most intriguing the first time I read *She* was that by identifying significant behavior patterns in myself, it meant that I had more control over my life than I had thought, and in a much more direct way.

During this time, my life was in relative chaos. The divorce process was under way; without an income, I needed to sell my house and move. And the longest I had known anyone in the area was a year. I ran out of money; I even got to the point that a repo guy called to warn me that he would have to pick up my car the next day if I didn't get current with the bank.

(I never heard of repo men doing that sort of thing, but I heeded the warning and didn't have to go out in the morning to find the car missing.)

Nothing I pursued professionally came to fruition. But occasionally I would be asked to do a small project, and that would lead to new people and other projects. Each job contributed something significant to my knowledge base, while keeping me relatively afloat financially. In the early Eighties, for example, I got familiar with the basics of computers through a marketing assignment for MicroPro.

There was never anything long-term or solid or lucrative, for most of the next fifteen years. I worked on projects involving corporate communications, public relations, and/or marketing. My range of subjects ran from notebook computers to video vending machines, medical equipment leasing to riverboat gambling, earthquake preparedness to taquerias. The longest I worked in one place was ten months. I sold cars, wrote books, and was briefly on unemployment. My favorite gig was directing a congressional campaign for four months.

While I always lived on the edge, I always had enough to eat, and to pay the rent though I was once ten days late. And I lived in some remarkable places. For 5½ months, for example, I was at Hurricane Point on the Big Sur coast, atop a 500-foot cliff overlooking hundreds of square miles of Pacific Ocean, my *backyard* filled with spouting whales, screeching hawks, and the light from the Point Sur Lighthouse which beamed through the living room windows every 15 seconds, when there wasn't too much fog. There was no phone for the first five weeks, and no electricity except for what was put out by a rarely-used gasoline generator.

Then there were 3½ years on Monastery Beach, in a wonderful old whaler's house, constructed in the 1870's using tree trunks for a foundation; sitting on a private acre in the middle of a state park, the beach twenty yards away, looking across Carmel Bay from Point Lobos.

(Sidebar: Housing has never been a problem for me. When I moved back to California in September of 1993. I arrived at five on a Friday afternoon. I started looking the next morning and had signed a lease for my new home, a lovely apartment overlooking San Francisco Bay toward Sausalito and the Marin Headlands, that afternoon.

I haven't always left much room for error. On one occasion, I was moving out of a house and didn't know to where. The movers had finished loading the truck, and I told them I'd give them directions in five minutes. Three minutes later, literally, a call came from a man who had been thinking of renting his house to me saying he'd decided "Yes."

Moving to Chicago a decade or so later, we found a place at eight o'clock the night before the movers were to arrive from the West Coast at eight the next morning.)

My home has been very important to me. I have needed that sanctuary – a place where I could feel safe and entertain the unsummoned thoughts that would appear – and I have always had that. Not lavish, but always secure. That I have found these places – some quite extraordinary, others simply comfortable – so easily when the rest of my life was in tatters was an indication to me that I was, in some way, not struggling on my own.

I wrote this book in a 400 square foot studio in the redwoods on a southeastern slope of Mount Tamalpais in Mill Valley. From my desk I could watch the sun rise over the opposite ridge through my east-facing windows. This home was the first classified listing I called about, and the first and only place I looked at, when it came time to move. It was also just a half-mile from where I first moved to California fifteen years earlier.

Is There a Why?

I have been writing since I was in my early teens; it has put bread on my table and brought peace to my mind. It may be genetic. My grandmother wrote for a Chicago newspaper in the Twenties. Her daughter, my mother, wrote a highly-respected newspaper column for *The Berkshire Eagle* (Pittsfield MA) and a number of books, one of which earned a National Book Award nomination. Two of my sisters have also written professionally.

I was first published in the *Daily Hampshire Gazette* in my hometown of Northampton, Massachusetts covering junior high school sports. When I got into television news a number of years later, I learned to write according to the rule that you "Tell 'em what you're gonna tell 'em, Tell 'em, and then Tell 'em what you told 'em." You need to do it that way, of course, because television is a strictly linear medium (unless you've taped a program and can replay it.)

In a book, you can read and re-read, but I haven't relied on that. I've attempted to present ideas with some degree of linkage. But with a story like this, there is no practical way to present all the ideas in a linear fashion; their inter-relationship is too complex. Like life.

While we live our lives in a time-linear fashion,

pulling off the calendar pages one after another, our acquisition of critical information is more amorphous than sequential. Certain thoughts are simple and clear. Some need to be repeated to take hold. Some ideas change context over time, with the assimilation of additional information and new perspectives.

It might help to read this book the way you might listen to a person whom you can't easily understand. Even if there is confusion at the outset, sometimes the meaning becomes clear when you listen longer and realize that the facts were there, just not in a sequence that was familiar to you. It's just one person's story, after all.

<u>Chapter One</u>

Is there a why? Well of course there is. But it's not something you believe or have faith in. It's something you know; you think It and you feel It. You have experienced It.

And if you're like me, you resisted It for the longest time. But then I had experiences that stretched the scientific *explanations* beyond reasonable bounds. Here are a couple of stories that pushed my limits.

*   *   *   *   *

– I was sitting with my friend Joan in the living room of our house on the cliff in Big Sur, talking about the clock on the wall above the sink in the kitchen. The minute hand was attached only by a small piece of duct tape, which, while efficient, was hardly aesthetic. My thought was that I should remove the minute hand because we didn't need it, since we stayed around the house most of the time and we could always guess the time within a few minutes by the position of the hour hand. A minute later I got up to get a glass of water. I walked across the unyielding stone floor to the kitchen where, when I was a few feet from the sink beneath the clock, the minute hand fell onto the counter.

– Another instance took place on Highway One along the Mendocino coast, late on a Tuesday afternoon, with no others cars on the road for minutes at a time. I was telling my friend Rita about the NEA funding issue and how there was a brouhaha over a grant to an obscure performance artist who was receiving taxpayer money to support an act which included urinating on stage on a picture of Christ. At that very moment, we came around a curve in the road, and there was a man urinating into the bushes. He had parked his car on the other side of the road, walked across to our side for no obvious reason, and was relieving himself in full view.

– A woman I hadn't spoken to in fifteen years – and haven't spoken to since – called me one evening just to say hello. In the course of the conversation, she mentioned her great pleasure with a science fiction writer named John Varley, of whom I'd never heard. This wasn't surprising since sci-fi wasn't a great interest of mine. After we had talked for over a half-hour, I returned to watching a videotape. When the tape ended and I turned the player to rewind, the television reverted to the station behind the tape player on channel three. They were showing a movie based on a short story by John Varley.

*   *   *   *   *

A number of years ago, when my friend Barry was in England, he got a call from Chicago informing him that his father had just died. Barry said he knew in that moment that he lifted the phone from the cradle that his father had died. How? I asked. I don't know, he said. He couldn't call it a coincidence, but he refused to entertain speculation about the intangible.

Most people have had similar if less dramatic experiences, or have heard personal accounts from otherwise-trustworthy friends of people simultaneously knowing of the death of someone hundreds or thousands of miles away.

(How is it that only that person who is supposed to get the message receives it? Why aren't the rest of us hearing it?)

Is *extraordinary coincidence* enough to explain such incidents? Or is there something connecting us that we aren't, for the most part, consciously aware of?

Most people, in contravention of the society's accepted view of reality, believe in ESP, UFOs, and angels; and the vast majority of people around the world believe in some sort of after-life. Is it out of a need to have a framework of belief; a spiritual element in one's life? Is it self-delusion? Or is it reality?

Are we bound for heaven or hell? Or another life? Or do we just die? For that matter, what are we now?

While some people point to religion and others prefer The Universe or The Cosmos to explain what is beyond their description. It seems that there is something bigger than ourselves, and I often refer whatever It is as a Larger Reality. (No capital letters; it's too big to need them.)

There must be a Larger Reality. Otherwise, what's going on? How else do we describe you and me in the here and now? It isn't plausible that your comprehension of this sentence is the result of some 15 billion years of random combining of amino acids and synapses to produce this moment together? (Did this moment merit that kind of preparation?)

Chapter Two

In journalism, even though Why usually produces the most interesting answer, it generally comes up last after who, when, what, where, and how. As regards this story of human beings and a Larger Reality, these other questions can be dispatched fairly quickly.

– Who is the human being generally, and those who are seeking greater understanding of the Meaning of Life in particular.

– When is now – the Atomic Age, the post-Sixties, the New Age, the verge of a new millennium.

– Where is the United States – the confluence of Western and Eastern traditions – and other non-geographic loci of evolutionary thought.

– What, I suggest, is a radical transformation of consciousness on the order of fish becoming amphibious.

– How is uniquely personal for each individual, but

seems to be a re-contextualizing of one's explanation of reality into a new and more functional framework.

(In journalism, there is also the question "So what," pertaining to the reader/viewer's interest. That blends into the "Why." As more people are deciding that their every-day lives seem to lack purpose, they are confronting a harsh, personal *So what*, which in increasingly more cases is promulgating searches like the one described in this book.)

Many people today are looking at their success and finding little satisfaction in it. Many others are wondering at their failure, and asking what is the point of it all. Teenagers are killing themselves at a rate three times greater than they were in the Fifties, in large measure because they are seeing a growing chasm between what society pretends is their future, and the dishonesty and hollowness of the picture.

The hunger to figure out our lives explains the large number of books and videos that offer alternative paths to erstwhile happiness. The self-help industry in the United States is over $11 billion a year.

Mostly the books and videos point to the fact that the answers are inside each of us, and that we have to follow the author's protocol to find them. It's simpler than that. You don't even have to ask for the answers, you just have to make yourself open to new information.

However, creating that *tabula rasa*, clearing our minds of all distractions, is the antithesis of the way we are living our lives at the end of the Twentieth Century. Rather, we fill our waking hours with input of every sort – the television is on an average of 35 hours a week (more than a quarter of our waking hours) – and then there's work and commuting and families and meals... when's a person to think?

For many people, the only time we have a chance to empty our minds is at night. When we are asleep and, perchance, to dream. Unfortunately, ours is a culture that doesn't recognize the importance for dreams.

(The only culture on the planet never to have fought in war, the Senoi of New Guinea, spends a great deal of time discussing their dreams, seeing dreams as an access to a higher level of being.)

Many people in our society even deny having dreams, as though it were something wrong; apparently everyone does, in fact, dream. Dream analysis is still pretty much considered fringe in Western culture, although it's gaining adherents in Jungian and other therapies, and in this (ever-extending) New Age, more people are keeping dream journals.

Dreams offer a wealth of images, many of which don't make sense in the context of our waking lives. We see places we've never seen, have relationships we wouldn't have, shoot guns that don't fire, fly without a plane, and succeed or fail on scales far grander than our waking imagination might ever entertain.

Where do those images come from? Who or what creates them in our minds? How and why do we remember the ones we do?

If we are so resistant to give credence to imagery that comes into our minds when we are as indeliberate about the process, such as sleeping, then perhaps it is because we don't consider it really safe to have uninvited thoughts come into our consciousness.

In his book *The Hitchhiker's Guide to the Galaxy*, one of Douglas Adams' characters observes that people on Earth seem to talk unceasingly, out of fear that if they stopped, they'd have to use their brains.

In the film *My Dinner with André*, Wally registers alarm at the idea of just sitting quietly. Why would I do such a thing? he asks. I'd pick up a book or talk to my girlfriend, shrinking from the very notion of having his mind otherwise dis-engaged.

The truth is that as a society we resist opening our minds to new concepts, and particularly to ideas so large that they threaten to dislodge our fundamental view of life; to untie our moorings. But that doesn't make those ideas go away. They are always there – like it or not; deny it or not – in multitudinous forms, waking and sleeping.

Not only do we not entertain new ideas, or deliberately not make room for them, we don't even ask where they come from. Remarkably little interest is paid to the origin of thoughts, where they come from, how they are summoned, and why we can't do a more effective job of managing their flow into our consciousness. Considering the amount of resources we spend on making our lives easier, little has been devoted to improving the efficiency of our own thought processes.

Take a mundane example. You drive down to the supermarket to pick up a few items. When you left the house ten minutes ago, you knew you wanted six things: bread, milk, butter, an onion, some apples, and potatoes. Now you're at the market. You remember that you came for six items and you've picked up five. But you can't for the life of you remember the sixth. You struggle and wrestle and look at the tip of your tongue...but nothing. Then, when you're standing in the check-out line, having given up remembering in disgust, you are distracted by the latest headlines in the tabloids. Suddenly the word "potatoes" pops into your mind.

Where did it come from? Why couldn't you *find* it when you tried? How is it that at times we can recall even the most obscure information from memory in a nanosecond, and at other times, we can't remember the name of a close friend?

How does information comes to the mind – on demand or unbidden? We know that we can deliberately solicit information that we have already processed, e.g., our telephone number, from our memory; at least most of the time. And we know that we can deliberately entertain new ideas, as, for instance, in writing a poem when we are looking for a rhyming word.

But sometimes we can't find information that we know we have stored, whether it be that item on the shopping list or the name of our fourth grade teacher. Indeed all too often we find ourselves searching for answers, at work or play, but they remain hidden from our conscious mind.

People who know the basics of how computers work will appreciate the numerous parallels in how information is processed by the human mind and, not surprisingly, by the machines the human mind designed to process information. For instance, we manage information in a short- and long-term form in our minds, as we have a file open on our desktop and saved onto the hard drive of a computer.

We also create filters in our thinking process in a fashion similar to how we might search for a piece of text; e.g., by date or geography or people in relation to that text. We sort through files with an extensive – one might say mind-boggling – capacity for cross-indexing. But note that while your computer can remember an old girlfriend's name, it can't remember the special look in her eyes or the smell of her hair.

The deliberate search for information, both stored and fresh, is a much less clumsy or haphazard process than most of us believe. There are various methods we can learn and develop to retrieve long-stored information and bring it to consciousness. And this fits into the common scientific explanation that these data are stored electro-chemically in our brains.

But where do new ideas come from? How does someone suddenly come up with a radical new discovery? Can we deliberately order up information that is in the public domain but that we have never personally processed, e.g., a Mozart concerto? And can we solicit information that is not yet (apparently) in circulation, like a cure for cancer?

Maybe.

Probably.

In all likelihood, all information is already available and we either aren't aware of it or are filtering it out unintentionally by looking only in the wrong places. The fact is that we are under bombardment by a limitless amount of information, but we are deliberately oblivious to it, focusing primarily on sensory information, perceiving little of that, and ignoring most of the rest. Of all that our eyes see, for example, our conscious mind sees about three-tenths of one percent.

Our mind, being significantly greater in capacity than in use, is inundated with a commensurate volume of thoughts of which the vast majority never make it to consciousness. People we call crazy are often victims of inadequate filtering, in terms of either volume or content or both. The rest of us, those whom we don't think of as crazy, manage to staunch the flow, operating if you will, an intellectual sphincter to protect ourselves from drowning.

My take on the process – without any formal scientific basis as far as I am aware – is that the right lobe of our brain operates as a receiver to the source of information – God, the cosmos, the collective unconscious – and the left lobe acts as the translator and editor. The left lobe, the thinking part of the mind, controls both flow and content.

The futurist and author George Leonard conducted some interesting demonstrations in his Energy Training classes, in which I participated, in the early Eighties. The classes were held in the Aikido of Tamalpais *dojo* (training center) in Mill Valley. One day, he had the 25 or so students standing around the mat close their eyes. He instructed that if someone were to feel a tap on the shoulder, he should open his eyes for the briefest possible moment to take a snapshot of what was before them and then close them.

After a few minutes, he told us to open our eyes and he went on to another exercise. Later, when the class was discussing the various exercises, he asked if anyone had anything to add. No one did. He smiled, not surprised, and said that during the time that we had had our eyes closed, he had gone a-round the room, and tapped four students on the shoulder. When he did so, he was standing in front of them wearing a garish mask.

Each of the four students then recalled the event, but none had thought to mention it. Why? George suggested that it was perhaps because what they saw didn't fit into there belief of what they were supposed to see. And, he noted that that is the way most of us live our lives, culling what is unfamiliar, unwelcome, and that which would separate us from the common group perception.

Indeed, most of us are living our lives out of habit. We don't even hear ourselves uttering the nonsense in much of our daily discourse. "Hihowaya?" is a greeting but not a question, like "Howzitgoin?" "No problem" instead of "you're welcome". And "Have a nice day" lost its meaning a long time ago; probably when the smile button came out.

Or consider the expressions "I don't care," "It doesn't matter," and "I have no choice". In truth, we really do care, it does matter, and we have made what we deem to be the best choice.

In fact, most of our thought processes, deliberate and incidental, are habitual. Deepak Chopra says that over ninety percent of the thoughts we have today we will also have tomorrow. And most of those thoughts, in the overall scheme of things, are extraordinarily banal; instructions in the operation of daily life.

This dovetails with scientific theory that we are using less than ten percent of our brains. And most of the limitations are due to social instructions, obeisance, and habit. In 1954, a number of scientific papers were published that said that it was physically impossible for a human being to run a mile in less than four minutes. That was the year that

Roger Banister broke the mark, and the following year another dozen people also clocked in under four minutes.

Or take the Olympic example of Bob Beaman who, in the 1968 games, broke the broad jump record, not by a quarter-inch, but by two feet. He ran, he jumped up, and for a while, he seemed to *forget* to come down. For a critical moment, he wasn't bound to the universally-held presumption that if someone were to break an Olympic long jump record it would be by a fraction of an inch. When asked how he did it, he said he didn't know, and he wouldn't try it again.

All of us are capable of significantly more than we are currently demonstrating. The capacity of our minds to produce is barely being touched. Nor is our ability to understand who we are, what we are, where we came from, why we are here, where we are going, and how we will get there.

Chapter Three

It's an over-used metaphor, but we might think of the flow of information to be like a river. If we could slice across the river, we would see all of that water, looking very much alike, as water molecules have a tendency to do. What we wouldn't be able see are the innumerable currents that were driving those individuals molecules.

If we were standing on the bank, we could observe a very small number of the currents operating on the surface. If we were standing in the river, we could feel some of the currents pressing water by us. But there is no way that we could see or feel or grasp the concept of all of the currents, let alone track the flow of the water molecules being moved by an infinite number of different currents. But we can still intellectually understand the difference between the water and the currents.

Thoughts are pressing themselves on our mind in a similar way. But we are confronted not simply by one river of information – even as broad and as torrential as one could possibly imagine. Rather, the flow is omni-directional. It is coming at us from all directions; from outside as well as from inside and through. We get new ideas from the outside, have feelings on the inside, and sense that we are in the middle of something going on between other sources.

Further, the human mind is capable of differentiating the water from the currents as it is differentiating ideas from their meanings and import. This selection process is a key to how our mind serves us. It is also how we are defined as human beings, to ourselves and to others.

The internet is an interesting metaphor. We have virtually all of the world's information available at our fingertips. Having access to all of the information, what will distinguish us from everyone else is what information we select and how we use it. (Sort of like everyone bellying up to an all-you-can-eat buffet; what you eat determines your physical well-being.)

Expanding on that image, who we are as a human being is defined by what we assimilate, how we manipulate it, and how we disseminate it.

The more we open our minds, the better we are able to reconstruct our assimilation process, to know better what information is available, and what to take in, what to do with it, and how to put it out.

But before you take the plunge and start demanding of the universe answers to pressing questions, both personal and global, there is a interim step that will offer some practical experience in the acquisition and management of new, unfamiliar, and unsolicited information. The reason why you may want to start here is to familiarize yourself with the flow, so that when you do start looking for stock tips or a recipe for the perfect marinade, not to mention a plan to end world hunger, you will be able to recognize the information that you seek.

Linguistically speaking, the first step is simple. Just unfocus your mind. Make room on your mental plate for a new image to appear. Stop thinking about work, about your wife, or that your car needs to be washed. Clear away all of your thoughts, and see what shows up. This may sound easy, but for anyone who has tried to meditate, it is really much harder than it seems. Thoughts come rushing in – Nature abhors a vacuum – and suddenly you will find yourself thinking about something. Anything.

You can train yourself to empty your mind. That's why they call meditation a practice. And you don't have to secrete yourself in a cave in Nepal for ten years to get there. It takes time to develop an open mind, but the more you practice, the more facile you will find the process. It's like relaxing against a muscle spasm. Instead of wrapping yourself in pain and tightening up against the spasm, you go inside of the pain and relax. The more you relax, the more the muscle will loosen.

So take a breath – a normal one; this isn't anything fancy – and clear your mind. It is often useful to focus your attention on your breathing; in through the nose, out through the mouth, in through the nose, out through the mouth; slowly, evenly, effortlessly. When a thought appears, push it out. And when the next thought appears, push that one away as well.

The more you push away your thoughts, the more likely it is that a new thought – a previously unthought thought – will manage to get through. Pushing away even just a few thoughts will dramatically increase the likelihood that a new and interesting thought – or a different perspective on a long-standing issue – will pop into your consciousness. Like somebody turning on a light.

You can try this as meditation, or sitting on a bus, or waiting in somebody's lobby. But as the ads mention, don't try this while operating heavy machinery. It may be too unfocusing an activity to try while driving. I've done it for years when I go for walks. I'll clear my mind deliberately and when I feel that I am adequately distracted from my normal course of thoughts, I'll often find that new images or perspectives will appear.

When something does capture my attention – e.g., hearing a bird screeching, seeing a familiar if unknown face, noticing a particularly oddly-shaped cloud – I will think about what it represents as an image; its characteristics rather than its fact. A bird may be soaring or diving or cruising; a face may be ethnic or emotional or aesthetic; a cloud may be soft, or white, or ominous.

Can you misinterpret the imagery? Yes, every time. Or sometimes. But not when you ask yourself freshly, without expectation or desire, what the object represents to you in that very moment. Because that's when you are perceiving it.

Let me restate this because it's important but not simple. When you see an image as it comes in for the first time, you are seeing it before the interpretive part of your mind has a chance to assess it. The right lobe has perceived it and you want to see it before the left lobe can define it for you. In that moment, the imagery is *pure*, untainted by judgment.

How do you know if you're judging it rather than seeing it? If you find yourself getting into an internal dialogue about what the image means, you may be past the point of receiving the information cleanly.

The more honest you are with yourself – the more willing you are to entertain the possibility of new, different, relevant imagery – the more likely you are to receive fresh and valuable information. As much as you might want to get a vision that endorses a path you have chosen, if you try to interpret the images to fit your own choices – to force the square peg into the round hole – you will necessarily be fooling yourself. Also, it will take you away from finding the correct interpretation. Whether you are working with the I Ching, Tarot or Runes, this approach to image interpretation is actually worse than useless because it will taint the very purpose of the interpretive process, on this occasion and in the future.

If there is a higher level of consciousness, if you can access it through a dialogue with your self, and if you attempt to do so motivated by a desire to grow, then it stands to reason that you will receive the information you need in a way that you can most effectively receive it. Don't use a cookie-cutter; instead, look at the shape of the dough.

There is no one to fool. No grades to skip. No one to get ahead of. You are conducting a unique, individual dialogue with our own source. Where would be the room – let alone the reason – for deceit, manipulation, or injury?

Oh, and the more you go this deeper-self route, the more often and quickly you will find answers to your questions. You will be acknowledged for your efforts and rewarded with information.

Chapter Four

What are we? In physical terms, merely a proto-plasmic upgrade from the zygote culture. What makes us different, and superior, to the other animals on the planet is our mind.

We don't have the flight of birds, the gills of fish, the speed of the cheetah, the power of the lion, or the communications of a dolphin, but we do have a unique intellectual faculty that allows us to acquire, interweave, and act on information. First it was critical to our survival, and now it is positioning us for attainment of a higher level of consciousness.

But what are we? A mind created from a mass of electro-chemical events? Or a body created by a mind? Which created which? Science says that the order is conception, birth, growth, and death, followed by decomposition of the body. That would imply that the mind is generated in the process of creating the body from the sperm and the egg, and dies with the body.

Hold that thought.

Is there a spirit (or soul or conscience)? The fact that we sometimes behave in ways that are not morally right, or even in our own personal best interest, is evidence that there minimally exists a dialectic between the determinant mind and a personal ethos. Is that moral force created by the mind, and if it is, what makes it different from the deliberate mind?

Wherever that spirit might come from, it appears with the mind and the body. Whether it pre- or ante-dates the person in life no one seems to know for sure. But if we accept the scientific view, the spirit is manifest by the mind which is generated by the body, or

Body > Mind > Spirit

So according to the scientific thesis, when the body dies there's no way for the mind to exist, and the spirit would consequently disappear.

When I was growing up, I didn't even think to separate the mind from the soul. The goodness, the essence, the substance of a person was in his character which was generated by the mind. The mind encompassed integrity, purpose, ethics, and conduct. If people used religion to induce higher levels of these qualities, well that was fine, too, although from my perspective religion was then being used as a something of a crutch.

We didn't hold crutches in high regard in my family, although we appreciated that others might need them, I always thought, stoically, that life would have been easier if I had believed in an afterlife; it would have been something to hold onto during those particularly trying times we experience in the pre-afterlife. But I didn't. I thought it was me and the world, and I had seen nothing to suggest otherwise.

Giving further thought to the Body>Mind>Spirit hypothesis, something just doesn't seem right. The body can live without the mind (brain-dead), but to what purpose? A mind can live in a crippled body and otherwise do quite well. And the spirit is clearly alive in the latter situation, and not apparent at all in the former.

Taking it a step further, we know that the body comes to an end and turns to dust; there is no evidence that the same thing happens to the mind. In fact, there are myriad cases of communications with minds of people whose bodies have been dead for years. That most are anecdotal is more a matter of the limits of science and professional imagination than a refutation of a vastly shared reality. And beyond those *conversations* with dead people, there are also the memories – a different sort of communication – that sometimes provoke deep sorrow, great joy, and new ideas.

There is also plenty of evidence of the universality of the spirit from (1) the common mythology and iconography in cultures around the globe, (2) the similar description of perhaps 75 million near-death experiences, and (3) the widely-held belief of a higher power despite a virtually complete lack of *tangible* proof of its existence.

Weighing these data, I have been drawn to the conclusion that the body is grown, managed, and driven by the mind; that the mind is part of that same force of co-incidence that brought together that sperm and egg, and began to build them into a body. That undefined force-energy-spirit then continues to operate through the mind and generates the entire physicality through a lifetime of maintenance, to a final breath.

Imagine this scene from a hospital movie...the patient on life support with all the incumbent wires and tubes, and the oscilloscope marking a wavy green line and beeping monotonously. Suddenly the line goes flat and the beeping stops; an alarm sounds. That's the signal that the energy system that has been running the body all this time – and which last act had been to make the line bounce and the beep – is no longer operating in that body. It has either ceased to exist or it has left the body, and so there is nothing to drive the oscilloscope.

This is demonstrable, measurable scientific fact; that's what the oscilloscope says.

Where does this unique energy system that created and ran the person come from, and where does it go?

Whatever the origin or destination, it is clear that something – god, coincidence, or what-not – causes the sperm and egg to get together, just as it is clear that when the body ceases to function, there is no longer the force in it to register on the oscilloscope. It is necessary, then, to infer that the relationship of body, mind, and spirit makes more sense if we turn the triptych around, and come up with a description that more functionally aligns with the facts; that is,

Spirit > Mind > Body

The Spirit, whatever its origin or purpose, generates the Mind which builds and maintains the Body. This construct also better follows the laws of physics dealing with energy and matter, (as far as I understand them through the writings of people like Stephen Hawking and Deepak Chopra). In terms of physics, it's more logical to think of energy consolidating purposefully to form a mind, than to think that one would be generated by matter spinning faster.

Physics is just an intellectual construct itself, based

on rational observation and assessment. And many times more people know of the existence of Spirit than have a clue about or an interest in physics. Physics may provide an explanation for the way things happen, but it is clearly the Spirit that makes them happen.

Whatever is the Spirit, we know It when we hear It in a child's full-throated laughter, see It in a lover's secret glance, feel It in the charisma of a true leader, and recognize It in the awakening to a new idea. It is a force greater than the mind; It uses the mind to implement Its purpose. In other words, the Mind is the interface between Spirit and Body.

*   *   *   *   *

Here's a different aspect of the discussion:

This transformation in which we find ourselves is about attaining a higher level of consciousness. The current phase that we are departing, which has lasted several tens of thousands of years, has been about creating a socio-mechanistic structure to sustain physical life, the Body.

We have now figured out how to supply food and build shelter to keep our physical beings functioning in an effective manner, even though we do not seem to be using this knowledge efficiently or compassionately. That plateau reached, we are about to embark on the next step, i.e., to see what the mind

is capable of, and purposed for, since we have attained the foundation level of physical survival.

<u>Chapter Five</u>

It was not so infrequent that when I walked through Tennessee Valley, a two mile trek through the Golden Gate Recreation Area to the Pacific, I saw a snake on the path in front of me. Did it mean something, anything? I didn't know, but I did think about it. I noted the thought I was having when the sight of the snake (always non-poisonous) captured my attention. I thought about the characteristics of snakes, their mythology and imagery, such as I know them.

(It didn't matter if my ideas were accurate as far as the facts were concerned. I made the association with my own imagery. Whether snakes represented cunning or fertility, the only association that counted was the one in my own mind at the time. It was I who saw the snake, and it was I who was making the connections.)

Then I thought about what relevance, if any, there was of those characteristics to what I was thinking about at the time the snake grabbed my focus. Did those archetypal references seem to color or direct what I was thinking about?

If not, I asked what else, if anything, in my life might that imagery be referencing? Inevitably, my mind found something to think about. It may have had nothing to do with the qualities of a snake, or have any connection to the interrupted thought. But I always did think about something new, or about something old with a new perspective.

Does that seem too obvious? Sometimes, the only function seeing that snake seemed to perform was to stop me from thinking about some particular issue; perhaps because I was taking my mind down a wrong road. Sometimes I found that the distraction served to shift my thoughts from an unproductive line of thought to a useful one. Maybe something new, or perhaps it was an issue I had been thinking about earlier, or chronically, and which had needed a new perspective.

Certainly no harm was done, unless I got so bogged down in contemplation and analysis that I stepped on the snake. (No, it never happened. I always kept a respectful distance.)

My experience was that the more I entertain the concept that what catches my attention is worth note – for its fact or its representation or its distraction – the more productive is my overall mental processing.

*   *   *   *   *

(Sidebar: At the moment my fingers were about to tap the keys, I received the following email from a friend of a friend who says it originated in Great Britain. It was titled *The Heavy Thinker*:

It started out innocently enough. I began to think at parties now and then to loosen up. Inevitably though, one thought led to another, and soon I was more than just a social thinker.

I began to think alone – "to relax," I told myself – but I knew it wasn't true. Thinking became more and more important to me, and finally I was thinking all the time.

I began to think on the job. I knew that thinking and employment don't mix, but I couldn't stop myself.

I began to avoid friends at lunchtime so I could read Thoreau and Kafka. I would return to the office dizzied and confused, asking, "What is it exactly we are doing here?".

Things weren't going so great at home either. One evening I had turned off the TV and asked my wife about the meaning of life. She spent that night at her mother's.

I soon had a reputation as a heavy thinker. One day the boss called me in. He said, "Skippy, I like you, and it hurts me to say this, but your thinking has become a real problem. If you don't stop thinking on the job, you'll have to find another job." This gave me a lot to think about.

Is There a Why?

I came home early after my conversation with the boss. "Honey," I confessed, "I've been thinking..."

"I know you've been thinking," she said, "and I want a divorce!"

"But Honey, surely it's not that serious."

"It is serious," she said, lower lip aquiver. "You think as much as college professors, and college professors don't make any money, so if you keep on thinking we won't have any money!"

"That's a faulty syllogism," I said impatiently, and she began to cry. I'd had enough. "I'm going to the library," I snarled as I stomped out the door.

I headed for the library, in the mood for some Nietzsche, with a PBS station on the radio. I roared into the parking lot and ran up to the big glass doors... they didn't open. The library was closed.

To this day, I believe that a Higher Power was looking out for me that night.

As I sank to the ground clawing at the unfeeling glass, whimpering for Zarathustra, a poster caught my eye. "Friend, is heavy thinking ruining your life?" it asked. You probably recognize that line. It comes from the standard Thinker's Anonymous poster.

Which is why I am what I am today: a recovering thinker. I never miss a TA meeting. At each meeting we watch a non-educational video; last week it was "Porky's." Then we share experiences about how we avoided thinking since the last meeting.

I still have my job, and things are a lot better at home. Life just seemed... easier, somehow, as soon as I stopped thinking.)

*　　*　　*　　*　　*

I have a rule that whenever I find myself thinking about something, I deliberately change the subject. I started this practice because I didn't trust myself. I thought that if I pondered something deliberately, I might come up with an answer that I wanted to hear, rather than get a clear, unprejudiced answer from... from wherever it is that ideas come from.

I maintain this practice, believing that while I can now effectively keep my Personality out of the analyzing process, that the fact of stepping out of the thought signals that thinking about it is no longer, at this moment, productive.

Our minds can juggle an amazing amount. There are dozens of dilemmas on the table, some serious and others that are not so important but which are basic elements in the average life, and that are in the forefront of consciousness. I can be thinking of a client's project, and my mind can jump to some new notes for an op-ed piece, or remember that I need to get my keys duplicated, or wonder what I should serve with the fish tonight, or that's a cute spaniel. Just for example. And it never ends, with most thoughts and thought lines looping through repeatedly and sometimes, when I'm procrastinating, annoyingly frequently.

What keeps all these disparate thoughts together is the same mind that is also moving my legs along the path, without stumbling into the sea or the path of on-coming dogs. It's the same mind that keeps me breathing, and relates me to the outside world through a smile of *hello* to other people on the path; not to mention, it's the same mind that is replacing zillions of cells in exactly the right way all the time to recreate 98 percent of my physical body in a year.

On a recent walk, I realized that I was not only singing quietly aloud, but I also had another, entirely different tune playing in my head. At the same time I was thinking about a work situation, and going back and forth about a number of personal issues...all the while managing to walk in a straight line without falling down.

We can take this for granted, of course, but at the same time we must marvel at our own unrealized – unimagined – potential. We know we are only using a small portion of our brain. What is it we don't know? How are decisions reached? And by whom?

If this sounds purely esoteric, try this. Sit down. Ask yourself a question. Any question.

Who decided what you would ask?

A part of your mind instructed that a question be

posed. Another part of the mind received the instruction and in some manner generated the question. Who are you having the dialogue with?

I first wrote about the multiple facets of the individual mind in 1985. When someone masturbates, one part of the mind asked another part of the mind to create a fantasy. At some point, presuming the mission was successful, the fantasy created by one part of the mind engaged another part of the mind and led it to a conclusion. I don't know if it was the first part of the mind, or a third part (and probably slower than the other two; or at least not as literary) but it's clearly more than one.

How many parts of the mind are there? How many different voices do we hear? Is it the same voice in a different tone? What about schizophrenics, or the murderers who claim that voices ordered them to kill?

Before trying to answer, consider another, more vigorous dialectic – that which exists between emotions and intellect; and how sometimes one erupts and/or the other freezes.

When I was writing the first chapter of this book, I hit a wrong key at the wrong opportunity and erased three pages and an hour's worth of work. I spent the next ten minutes trying to find even a scrap of the file. None was to be found.

This wasn't the first time that such an apparent catastrophe had occurred, although it hadn't happened in years. And when I did something like this, or if I had lost something (another uncommon event), I realized that I didn't need the thing anymore. In the case of a file, I knew – more than a rationalization – that I could improve upon what I had written. Or in the event of a lost jacket, for example, someone else probably needed it more than I did; and it gave me an excuse to get a new one.

Thinking something is not the same as feeling it. I was furious at what had happened. I focused my anger on the computer, and the new word processor I was using. Had I been working in the old software, I could have recovered, at least most of the work. If the new software could do the same, I didn't know how.

I shouted a clipped obscenity at the universe, and sent some really angry feelings toward whatever it is that did that to me. I looked down at the innocent keyboard and imagined smashing my fist down upon it.

I also watched myself having this tantrum. No, I didn't smash the keyboard, or anything else. And the one swear was enough. But I was still angry and resentful. And I allowed myself to feel this way for a while. The feelings didn't feel good; in fact I felt awful, but that was the familiar place of feelings and behavior patterns that I went to inside myself when something stupid and unnecessary happened.

Frustration and fury from one part of my mind, allowed to vent by another part of the mind that limited the form of the anger. Nothing broken, nothing hurt. Maybe a little self-opprobrium at getting so upset, or in thinking that swearing would somehow help.

(Sidebar: Later that evening, when I was over my snit and feeling better, my friend Mary-Jo called and was very sympathetic about what had happened. And then she offered another perspective. She said that such losses were (1) karma for something wrong I'd done, and (2) a reminder not to be attached to anything – text, ideas, or people. I heard and understood what she was saying, but it was too New Age-y for me. I felt some annoyance rise...that I then laughed at.)

How do we actually think? One way is to start with an idea, respond emotionally to the idea, and then instigate thoughts to unfold through that emotional over-lay. If I'm in a sour mood, I view both the people and the ideas I bring to mind negatively. Negatively inclined, I may bring to mind people who have let me down, or projects that aren't working optimally.

If I am in a good mood, however, the people and events and ideas are positive in themselves and/or are illuminated in a positive light.

That may seem obvious to the point of trite, but there certainly are a lot of people who allow themselves to make serious decisions about important issues while clearly in an emotionally off-balance – angry or giddy – frame of mind.

This is a glimpse of some of what makes the framework of emotion and intellect so fluid, demanding, and influential. And it is just one of numerous bifurcation in the mind's structure.

But is it another dialectic? Or is there another aspect between emotion and intellect, perhaps one that arbitrates between the two?

What else do we experience besides emotion and intellect? What is intuition? Where do the senses fit in? What about subjective and objective? Who holds judgment, and what happens when morality conflicts with law? How is it possible to be gloomy on a beautiful day, and who decides?

Whew!

Lately I've being feeling overwhelmed. There's too much to think, and think about. I sometimes doubt that I can handle so many thoughts; the panicky voice is warning "Overload!"

Is There a Why?

Which is why I am so willing – indeed, at times, anxious – to be distracted by a snake, a pelican, a vista, or someone else on the path.

Chapter Six

What is the Mind? It is the communication structure between Spirit and Body; it is the operating
system of the human being. It jump-starts the person, grows it to full form, and attends to all of the
plumbing, wiring, maintenance, repairs, et cetera,
for the physical life.

It also generates the personality.

David Spangler, one of the Findhorn founders,
noted that the first awareness of a human being is
of existence. Then it perceives Other, distinguish-
ing it from Self.

The Self – the individual incarnation or manifesta-
tion of Spirit – creates through the Mind an interface with Other. We call this interface the Personality (or the Ego).

The Person(ality) we present to the world is the
creation of the Self, and though sometimes our
Personality seems to appear to be in control, the

actual hierarchy is otherwise and definitive, though not always exercised.

In the Bergman film *Autumn Sonata*, a character says, "I could always live in my work but never in my life." It works as a metaphor about Self and Personality. While most people do, for the most part, live in their Personalities, it is a matter of choice, usually funded by habit, fear, ignorance, or lack of consciousness.

And since virtually everyone is living in their social interface, it's difficult to find people anxious to drop their masks. To remove the interface, to end the posturing, would mean revealing one's Self, and that is mostly discouraged in society. The public attitude, deeply ingrained, is that it is more important to be part of the majority than it is to acknowledge seeing the truth. Most people have been living with this choice for so long – as long as they can remember, even if they do remember making the choice – that they usually can deny, even to themselves, that they see an alternative.

Consider, you wake up in the morning and from your earliest moment of consciousness, you put on your personality. Like a body-stocking, except that it masks your Self with a your Personality. That presentation is the same person you showed yesterday. Little, in most lives, changes in deed or in thought. And so, we become more ever more deeply invested in, and committed to, a reality of our own construction.

From the moment of your arrival, and likely before, it is presumed that, regardless of your deepest thoughts and feelings, you will design and generate a personality that will satisfy the requirements of the society.

The foundation of the personality is usually created in the home through the instruction, and under the supervision, of the parents. The rest of the societalization takes place in school, in social and civic relationships, in church, and in the workplace.

Those who refuse to play by the rules – the people who present themselves in a role that contravenes the accepted standards – are ostracized as criminals or sociopaths in one direction, and as saints and eccentrics (and artists) in an opposite direction.

To preserve itself as an entity, society has resisted change at almost every opportunity, employing the threat of ostracism to coerce subservient participation by its individual members. When society lags necessary updating of its tenets, increasing numbers of their members find themselves marginalized, if not overtly, than at least in their internal commitment to participate. The longer the society holds off modernizing, the more people find themselves just managing to hold on; and others have already *quit.*

Many of the principles that proscribe public conduct are anachronistic, at best, and the lack of their application tends to create chaos. And chaos undoes stability, which is the primary purpose of a society.

With (1) people living longer, (2) forced assimilation of and association with more and diverse micro-societies, (3) a collapse of the institutions, and (4) the end of noblesse oblige, more people come to the realize that the emperor isn't wearing any clothes.

A witness to – and sometimes a collaborator with – the increasing shredding of the social fabric has been the creation, rise, and decline in psycho-social therapy. Initially it was suspect, then it became accepted, then chic, and finally, in large measure, irrelevant. I say this with honest deference to my father and others who have nobly practiced a profession which tried to make people more effective in – and feel better about if possible – performing their roles in society.

Unfortunately, the formula of most therapy is to induce an individual to conform his behavior to the social norm. There is rarely any exploration of whether the individual person might be right and society is out of whack. The inherent, foundation presumption is that the individual needs to be *fixed* because he is alone and cannot survive without acquiescing to – at least in appearance – the group think.

Jung put it this way:

Psychoanalysis cannot be considered a method of education if by education we mean the topiary art of clipping a tree into a beautiful artificial shape. But those who have a higher conception of education will prize most the method of cultivating a tree so that it fulfills to perfection its own natural conditions of growth.

As the number of people who were having trouble staying within the antiquating boundaries grew visibly and rapidly, therapists began marketing *cures* in the form of blame-shifting and concomitant victimhood. Suddenly, no one had to be responsible for his actions, and everyone was owed something by society. The tab grew too heavy, generated opprobrium at the excess, and the pendulum began swinging back toward personal responsibility.

Most people are willing to go along; for the most part, most of the time. Most people don't allow themselves to even think about challenges to the social order; by others, and certainly not by themselves, at least publicly.

This may account for much of the substantial stress

and reliance on prescription drugs like Prozac among the upper and middle classes; the lower classes are expected to be stressed, and turn to alcohol and drugs when they can't cope. But millions of seemingly-normal people are struggling with the conflict between the joined societal *reality* and the gnawing feeling that they themselves are not on the right page. The greatest stress comes when they have to deal with the feelings and thoughts that they don't know if they could change – go along or *find themselves* – to live satisfactorily in their society-required personality...even if they wanted to.

There is no question but that some competent therapists have provided their clients with useful, sometimes vital, perspectives on their behavioral patterns; offering illumination into darker recesses of early confusion. But for the most part, therapists are like auto mechanics working for an airline; they are great at keeping the wheels and brakes in order, but they can't do much about getting the planes into the air.

We all live in our Personalities, perhaps more than we prefer; there are few waking opportunities to do otherwise. It's difficult even to imagination what kind of communication would go on between two people who took off their masks with each other. That's what intimacy is about, and for most people heavily into their personalities, it's a very scary place to approach. Certainly not an arena for which we are prepared; in fact, we are trained only to perform through Personality.

Of course, an objective view is that the less Personality we put on, the healthier and more honest must be our relationships. The thinner the veil, the less obtrusive the interface, and the richer the connection between Self and Other, or Spirit and Spirit. And with our deepest creative Self squandering less time in (and generating) the Personality, the more time is freed for other, truly interesting exploration.

Chapter Seven

We need more perspective on the relationship between the Self and the Personality.

As a first stage, the Self begins creating the Personality as the connection with Other through the
stimulus-response communications that take place
in the first months of infancy. In a healthy environment, the new creature will learn a set of signals to
obtain food, burping, changing, loving, et cetera.
Then it will move on to walking, talking, toilet
training, and pre-school. By the time the child is off
to grammar school, around age six, his Personality
has essentially been formed.

Most of the behavioral changes that take place in
adolescence and early adulthood ratify and reinforce that communication system that we see as the
Personality. So with some fine-tuning here and
there, it is this Personality – this communication
system between Self and Other designed for the
purpose of satisfying the most basic needs – that is

with that person throughout his life.

By the time a young adult has grown into a *full-fledged* member of society, the Personality has been codified, ingrained, and ossified by almost twenty years of exposure to the elements of society. Why would anyone think of changing? What would cause a person to look at himself and say, I'm not sure this is really working; I think I'll make a new me.

(Sidebar: One night, on a first date, I asked the woman if she were asking herself if I were real. It may sound presumptuous, but it wasn't meant that way. I didn't even think of the question before I asked it. And though startled, she answered "Yes." I responded, "Yeah, who would choose to present me this way?" Neither of us had an answer to that, though she laughed and felt off the hook.)

Mostly, the question never comes up. Since the Personality was designed and installed under a rather primitive circumstances for the purpose of basic survival, it fits snugly next to the Self. It *protects* the Self from both the known and the unknown, based on what information was available at the time the Personality was fashioned. (The *inner child* is such a popular figure these days because it was he, so innocent, who was cocooned at that early age.)

The Personality does a remarkable job of managing relations with Other and should not be summarily dismissed, even if many aspects of it are anachronistic and unyielding to new circumstances and needs. As popular as ego-bashing is today, remember that it was the Personality that enabled us to join society instead of being institutionalized as an outcast. It was our Personality that generated, for better or worse, our relationships – between our Self and Other – created and honed our reputation, and managed our comportment and general presentation.

Studies say that the Personality is probably 90% set by age five in a child brought up in a healthy home. In a less healthy – less safe – situation, it is formed earlier for defensive purposes.

Since Personality is formed primarily by need, children brought up in safe and nurturing environments tend not to need to create as protective a shell; such as might be needed and created by an abused or deprived child. As the children from those two different environments grow up, the safer one will be less encumbered and will be better able to fine-tune his Personality; the suffering child will be editing his Personality through a thicker barrier.

(Sidebar: I have struggled to find an image that properly represents the Self creating the Personality. When I first tried to explain my perception of the Self and the Personality, I offered the image of a bubble of heat rising to the surface of a thick soup (without bursting); that is, the heated air being the Self and the bubble of soup around it the Personality.

And then I thought of the carnival game in which I fired a water pistol at a clown figure; when I hit the target of the clown's mouth, it forced compressed air into a balloon on top on the clown's head. The person who shot best and forced the most air into the balloon most quickly won when the balloon burst.

Both of these images fail. Perhaps a better one would be the story of the ventriloquist's dummy who takes control of its creator.)

The Self launches and maintains the Personality, although it soon appears unable to contain it, except catastrophically. The demands of Other, the society, force the Personality to perform in ways that are usually not fulfilling to the Self, but necessary for participation in the social structure.

To say that the Personality takes charge usually does not overstate the case. The Personality dominates waking life; it makes sure that it is constantly engaged, and thus needed. In that process, the presence, identity, and purpose of the Self is diminished. For some personalities, who have managed to ignore and/or deny the Self, the only contact with it may be in their dreams.

More and more, however, it seems that people are being confronted by their true Self(s). Usually it is in a time of crisis or chaos, when the ability to exercise what we call Self control but is really Personality control, seems to slip. A door opens to alternative perceptions, and suddenly the person is confronted with the fact of the Self-Personality dialectic.

I think what enlightenment is about is looking down through one's Personality and into one's Self. Like seeing one's face in the mirror and suddenly looking into the eyes, those windows to the soul, and realizing that there is more beyond the image. Much more.

Perhaps it is the Spirit that is the light at the end of the tunnel; the darkness being the Personality. Maybe enlightenment is glimpsing, just for a fraction of a second, that source of our Self, and in that moment, revealing a bit of insistent truth to the Personality.

Seeing that light, whatever it may be, is an indelible experience. We know, at least intuitively, of its significance. As we grow into social structure – through adolescence and young adulthood – the more social demands we engage, and the more we look and reach outward, away from the Spirit source; the further we solidify our protective layer, the less likely we are to look back, inside. So it is not until we are much older, when seeing that light – our forgotten Self – is a surprise, that we experience a jarring sense of reconsideration.

Some people don't understand the value of and need for the Personality and try to destroy it, which, conceptually, seems impossible. But clearly, the less Personality that exists, the more flexible, spontaneous, and true will be the Self's relationship with Other.

Just as it is easier for a diver to move around wearing a wetsuit and tank rather than a clunky deep sea diving suit and helmet (attached to the surface – society – for survival by tubes and cables), so is a person more adept at interaction and more effectively able to cope with surprises *wearing* a less cumbersome interface.

Enlightenment – becoming aware of the existence of Self and the concept of Personality; acknowledging the dialectic – is not in itself enough to draw down the Personality. In fact, this awareness is most likely to trigger a powerful defensive response by the Personality, taking the form of fear, anger, hostility, and denial. Understandably, since witnessing the light, seeing the greater realm, necessarily threatens the Personality's position; if not its very existence. At least in the Personality's survivalist view. The Personality is forged out of necessity, as a bulwark against Other, and its first function is survival.

More people these days are awakening; having a personal experience that causes them to question their own lives. Sometimes it is a positive experience, but it seems that most people I've met have opened themselves to this experience out of frustration and despair. It may be that this is an evolutionary stage in the species that instigates the questioning of the perceived reality. To some, I think, it could be that society's failure to hold up its side of the bargain – security, a valid dream, and a sense of belonging in return for participation – may indeed signal a fundamental, wholesale rupturing of the basic social contract.

It might also be seen that the schism between the individual and the society that it creates, parallels the difference between the Self and the Personality. The Self creates the Personality, and the Personality takes control, just as the society is created by individuals and exists only with the concordance of the individuals. When the Self and the individual show signs of his own life, the Personality and the society panic.

Which would certainly explain conditions today. In

the world's richest society, a third of the children live in poverty. Hundreds of thousands of people are homeless. Our institutions – education, health care, criminal justice, the economy – are so far out of balance with fairness and purpose that they openly and increasingly fail to serve the needs of the society. The standard of living for 80% of the population has been stagnant or worse for the past four decades.

If you lost your job and couldn't feed your children, what laws and obligations to society would you consider important? Wouldn't you fall back on yourself to de fine new parameters of behavior?

Chapter Eight

Concomitant with my personal voyage has been the observation of a vast decline in the social structure of our democratic republic. The public has stopped participating to any significant degree in the political process. Barely half the populace eligible to vote does so, and only a small, wealthy elite is involved in the selection of the candidates.

Meanwhile, the public wants fiscal responsibility, social conscience, campaign reform, and protection/restoration of the environment. The two major political parties represent decades of fiscal mismanagement, and failure in dealing with such societal problems as housing, health care, food, education, transportation, guns, campaign reform, safe streets...the list is long and tragic.

If our problems could just be written off as the failure of incompetent politicians, it might be acceptable, but we've been doing that for too long, and are now approaching the point of no return;

where if we don't act to change our course in a major way, the destruction of the environment could literally threaten the continuance of the species. Recognition of this fact – if only on a visceral level – especially by people who love and are worried for their children, is raising the general level of concern, but those controlling our lives – corporate leaders in collaboration with political leaders – are heading us in the opposite direction.

Either fear about the situation is contagious, or a lot of people are making the same assessment, and the degree of concern by thinking (vibrant) people is becoming palpable.

What is it that is happening now, for the first time in the past fifteen or so thousand years of *civilization*?

What happens when the social compact shatters?

For the past nearly half-century, since around the time of Apollo 13, the invasion of Cambodia, and the killings at Kent State, we have been in a serious moral decline. Money has bought power, and greed has taken control. We talk very little to each other, and when we do, it's often about something we saw on television.

Parents are publicly admitting that they don't know how to raise their children. People are running red lights as if they were living in a video game. And it is chic to disrespect our own, democratically-elected government. We loudly acclaim our country as the greatest democracy on earth, and as proudly trumpet our decision not to vote.

This schizophrenia is far more than a political statement; it is a rejection of the social structure. No wonder the Republicans were able to find such a responsive chord when they started talking about family values. The values that used to define us as a society are no longer being passed on. It wasn't that long ago that it would have been unacceptable to sport a bumper sticker saying "Shit Happens." In San Francisco in 1996, the newspapers and television stations showed photographs of Richard Allen Davis, the convicted murderer of Polly Klaas, *flipping off* the jury, the family, and the media; on the front page, and in slow motion.

Charles Silberman, who studied criminality, said that we are failing to societalize. He told of the experience on a minesweeper in the Pacific toward the end of the Second World War. While Germany was still fighting, there was very little rotation of the crew. Everyone on board understood the rules of their ship-board society: you used water sparingly, and you didn't steal. A sailor could leave a pack of cigarettes on his bunk and it would be untouched.

But when Germany stopped fighting, the rotation of crewmen became faster. There were fewer old guys to show the new guys the ropes. Soon, water was being wasted and it was not longer safe to leave a pack of cigarettes on your bunk.

Similarly, now in our general society, with women having left the home for the office or factory, parenting has been left to day-care centers and television; there is no one creating a social-sacred foundation of responsible understanding and participation. We are not passing on the lore, the myths, the codes, the standards, the directions, the hope.

For that is what is at the crux of the epidemic fear. It is not about the facts of the hundreds of thousands of manufacturing lay-offs or the pending collapse of the Social Security system. It is not about the statistics on murders or SAT scores, or the headlines about the incompetence and depravity of our political leaders. It is deeper, much deeper. America is in crisis because of the perception – intuitive, and now more cognitive – of a crucial lack of moorings, and little sign of reason to hope for positive change. As the old joke goes, the food is lousy, and the portions are small.

It is this sense of abandonment that is forcing people to stifle their fear with drugs and alcohol, to seek refuge in ardent religion or cultism, or to try to outrun the tsunami of public debt and global weaponry by amassing personal wealth and power; presuming that these will matter.

Some people intuit that the old ways won't work; that this time, it won't be a matter of changing parties or even governments. It won't be external affiliations that count. Fritjof Capra said in *The Turning Point* that at times of transformation, the world seems to spin faster; to many people, life looks out of control. People who can't maintain their balance may fly out to the fringes. Which explains the large numbers claimed by the religious right, and the rise to strident visibility of the anti-government militia movements.

These conditions point to a key question about this massive shift in our social structure. Can we survive it? If we bifurcate – if we boil it down to the people who want a just world against the people who have the guns and money – it will be a very ugly scene. How can it be avoided? Since the people who have the guns and money will not willingly relinquish either, and since an attempt at confiscation or confrontation would be lethal, the only practical alternative is to arrive at a circumstance whereby the guns and money would lose their power and value.

But what would be worth more than guns and money?

What if people who reach a higher level of consciousness would be able process information to effect more efficiently than would people who merely held sway through arms or wealth?

In *The Celestine Prophecy,* James Redfield hugely popular novel worldwide in the mid-1990s suggested that it was a higher level of consciousness – a higher vibrational level – that was the next step io our evolution.

A higher vibrational level? What does that look like?

Perhaps we can't know, yet. Can you explain sight to someone who has been blind from birth? Or sound to a deaf person? Or intuition to a strict constructionist?

*   *   *   *   *

It may be that the chaos that has grown dramatically since I first wrote this book 22 years ago is an indication that we are on the verge of a social transformation on the level of the fish climbing out onto the land. With much of the confusion and anger found in the declining intelligence and rising immorality of the religious zealots and anti-intellectuals, progressives are being challenged to hold on to what has been achieved in human rights and environmental protection and restoration.

Most key is that the presumed gold standard of

right vs. wrong seems to be dissolving, particularly for those with money and guns, which means that in a confrontation, the white hats are in trouble. This outlook has particularly darkened since the election of Donald Trump who has vigorously enfranchised the worst in us.

Chapter Nine

The problem with trying to sense – see, feel, taste, hear, smell – a higher level of consciousness is that it's probably not sense-able. We can't see ultraviolet light, hear a dog whistle, or touch a hologram. And yet, if we make the presumption that there is some larger, over-riding system or power, why do we think we should be able to perceive it with the society-colored glasses that we have been wearing without question for all of our lives? Why should there have been no validation of such reported over the millennia of our history?

The mono-theist god – the fellow in the long white robes that seems to be the popular image in this country – doesn't seem to encompass or explain enough, perhaps because he's been too anthropomorphized; god is too man-like, if you will. I've never gotten the part about we are supposed to be made in his image; ergo, god must be a singular being, albeit powerful, and that his faculties are our faculties only broader and stronger.

And as all powerful as this god might be, how is it conceivable that he is watching everyone in every life? There are, after all, more than seven billion people on this planet. And even if he only watched the Christians, one day of rest a week wouldn't be enough.

Another problem with the Judaeo-Christian explanation is that if there was such a being, you'd think he would have made another appearance by now. How much uglier do things have to get? Why wouldn't a supreme being do a couple of tricks to get the evil-doers (back) in line?

Or are things on this planet so bad right now that it's implausible to believe in any kind of benevolent higher power? The Holocaust, the Stalinist purges, 220 million people killed in wars in this century; how could anyone or thing allow these things to happen? And if god didn't show up to stop these events, well, wouldn't it be hard to believe that any larger presence exists?

*   *   *   *   *

I think there is a larger system; that it is apparent; and that we overrate the importance of much in our lives; e.g., things, relationships, goals, accomplishments. This becomes obvious when you work it backward. Which is what is happening to a lot of people. Their lives don't seem to be working, in one way (or many); what they thought was important doesn't seem to be, or as much; and nothing has come in to fill the void of missing purpose. Why are we here?

Confronting this void generates a deep sense of loss; something is missing; we are drowning in an abyss of alienation and aloneness. Often there is an urge to chuck it all and start over, maybe somewhere less populated, or at least in a situation that is less stressful.

Depending on your state of mind and frame of reference, you are likely to find, increasingly, that the description of reality under which our society is operating doesn't fit as well as you thought it did. Some of the rents in the fabric reveal significant discrepancies between beliefs and the facts.

Faced with the dispiriting discovery that you're in the middle of a herd of cattle heading for a cliff, you wonder if you really wanted to wake up to this. Are there other people out there who know what's going on? Are they willing to talk about it? Well maybe, but denial is rampant – both in themselves, and especially toward others – and is usually cloaked in apathy or the mindless nouveau-chic, "My vote doesn't count." Press the question with them, and they stop returning your phone calls.

The New Age, as it is benignly referred to, is not just a fad. It is the dawning of what Einstein called "a new way of thinking." He said,

The most beautiful emotion we can experience is the mystical. It is the power of all true art and science. He to whom this emotion is a stranger, who can no longer wonder and stand rapt in awe, is as good as dead. To know that what is impenetrable to us really exists, manifesting itself as the highest wisdom and the most radiant beauty, which our dull faculties can comprehend only in their most primitive forms – this knowledge, this feeling, is at the center of true religiousness. In this sense, and in this sense only, I belong to the rank of devoutly religious men.

What is evolutionary about this shift in how we think is that while a large group may be doing it, everyone is doing it alone. Not that there isn't plenty of discussion going on about it, and books and lectures and workshops; but for all of the talk and instruction, looking inside yourself and discovering your own Self is an individual journey.

It's not a matter of searching for something outside, or even for something sense-ably tangible.

There are two ways to conceive of the existence of something you can't perceive directly. One is to see the results, e.g., Big Foot's footprints. A second way is to develop a non-sense, i.e., intuition. Being then able to triangulate your knowledge between the thinking (seeing the signs) and the feeling (intuitive) parts of your mind, you can, with your determinant mind, create an internal hologram of sorts, that while not tangible to the senses is perceivable to the mind. The formula is

To Think + To Feel = To Know

Chapter Ten

The learning process is amorphous because it involves both sense and non-sense, intellect and emotions, the cognitive and the intuitive mind. Information can come in more than once, and take root, or uproot, and in different ways. Sometimes it is not the information itself that is so important, as the process of learning it.

About all anyone can do for another in this process is to share hand-holds of an intellectual variety that have helped to clarify or that have stimulated thought in a productive direction. Of particular value to me have been the books by Robert A. Johnson, especially *She* and *Transformation*; early Deepak Chopra videos; *The Power of Myth* with Bill Moyers interviewing Joseph Campbell; and the film *My Dinner with André*.

These sources offered particularly valuable pieces of information to creating and refining a framework that for me provides an explanation for the various questions that challenge the primary religious and scientific explanations for this life. But such reference points are only one, albeit critical, part of the process of building a new, complete perspective.

Using the formula that knowledge requires both thought and feeling, such intellectual explanations invite and require an intuitive complement. And accessing the intuitive complement, at least initially, is not made through focused effort; on the contrary, my experience is that the only way to let the intuitive *feelings* come through is to relax the deliberate mind.

You may also discover that those intuitive feelings have been there all along – some vying for attention, and others received but mis-interpreted. At first, it seems impossible to *order up* particular information from your intuitive mind, but two things are happening. One is that we often are asking for the wrong information, and another is that we are often getting the right information but are not recognizing it. (Later, it becomes possible to dialog with the intuitive and to successfully invite comment on an issue.)

Too often, however, we don't listen effectively, or we reject a clear answer if it's not what we want to hear. (My friend Mary-Jo would meditate until she got a headache if what she was hearing didn't conform to what she wanted. Once, she admitted, she went through her Tarot cards five times until they equivocated slightly from giving her the same answer, one she didn't like, to one that was indeterminate enough to regard as connoting what she sought.)

For the most part, I've stayed away from dialoging because I haven't been fully clear that what I was *hearing* wasn't being colored by my own Personality. I might even hear something that I wanted to hear – something that would make me feel better – but I would reject it out of hand for that reason.

Over the past three years, I've discerned a significantly different quality to the way I received information that I needed. It would arrive in an especially clear and vibrant way, completely and obviously detached from my other, more familiar and relatively-lackluster thoughts. The new information would invariably be about something creative – sometimes work-related, other times having to do with some fiction I was writing, or with a relationship – and would resonate with its own extra-ordinary value to the point that I might stop walking and remark on it aloud, as the idea percolated and shone.

It's a very exciting moment, processing and reviewing a strong new idea; celebrating its scope and glory. This isn't, of course, on the order of a cure for cancer or ending violence in the Middle East. But in that moment of discovery, you know that this brilliant idea or plotline or marketing design comes from that special place on the other side of the mental horizon. Such an experience reinforces the wisdom that sources from beyond consciousness (un-, non-, sub-, nearly-conscious); those ethers where ideas come from, is far more accessible and for far more significant information than most people realize.

For all of the excitement and the brilliance of the light, it is not about ownership of the ideas. The feeling of bringing forth significant information is the experience of being well-used. It is very deep and personal; the antithesis of seeking external approval. It is having a sense of internal validation beyond what any other person could accord.

George Bernard Shaw declared so poignantly,

This is the true joy of life, the being used for a purpose recognized by yourself as a mighty one, the being a force of nature instead of a feverish, selfish little clod of ailments and grievances, complaining that the world will not devote itself to making you happy. I am of the opinion that my life belongs to the whole community, and as long as I live, it is my privilege to do for it whatever I can. I want to be thoroughly used up when I die, for the harder I work, the more I live. I rejoice in life for its own sake. Life is no 'brief candle' to me. It is a sort of splen-

did torch which I got hold of for the moment, and I want to make it burn as brightly as possible before handing it on to further generations.

One doesn't have to go outside or be involved in a particular activity to experience such moments of clarity and purpose; indeed, good ideas pop up during a quiet meditation or in the midst of desperate circumstances. Invention can be born by the mother called necessity, but also by she of the peaceful empty mind.

Deepak Chopra says, the more we put ourselves close to Nature, the more we are getting closer to our own same source. If you presume that what we call life in ourselves and in plants and animals is essentially the same, then it stands to reason that we are more in our own element when we are with plants and animals instead of televisions and buses.

Much of the insight I've gained has come during the hour-plus walks I try to take every day, usually alone, when I make a concerted effort to keep my mind clear. Morning, lunchtime, late afternoon – it doesn't so much matter the time as the fact that I remove myself from the stimuli of the computer screen, telephone, and the pile of notes and folders taking over a corner of my desk.

My walk would usually take me by a part of San Francisco Bay or to the Pacific Ocean at the end of

Is There a Why?

Tennessee Valley Road in Mill Valley; now it's mostly Carmel Bay. I will invariably see shorebirds and flowers. Perhaps it seems hackneyed, but by noticing these co-vivants operating with the same life source – *stopping to smell the roses* – induces a conjoined sense of awe and appreciation. That is the cognitive perception.

The intuitive complement is the feeling of oneness, peace, and purpose. I feel a certain resonance, a sense of participation, that expands inside as I let my thoughts of the day dissipate.

It is not only the glory of the day – the sun, the colors, the freshness of the ocean breeze – there is also the wonder of it all. The other afternoon, as I was walking along the Tiburon bike path that winds around a small piece of The Bay, I was thinking about this writing, and I asked my Self what would be evidence of the existence of a higher order, and suddenly these words came into my mind:

What is the point...of the flowers and the birds, music and laughter, creativity and love? Why is it here, doing itself? What is the meaning – not of mine alone – but of life itself on this Earth?

I took three more steps and stopped to write this:

You cannot simply infer that as you taste the anchovies in your Caesar salad tonight while delighting to the

sounds of Lorraine Hunt singing Handel's arias, and
later self-intoxicating with the hint of the exotic scent on
your wife's shoulder, watching as the smoldering inter-
est in her eyes flames into passionate necessity, touching
each tender moment with the tips of your fingers and
tongue....Can you really tell me that the Universe, after
some fifteen billion years of indeliberate evolution, has,
through mindless opportunistic electro-chemical reac-
tion and sheer coincidence, created this evening without
rhyme or reason?

Sometimes it's easy to let one's Self flow into ink.

There are other, related reasons for taking the
walk. One is that it affords me the opportunity to
meet people. Sometimes I will run into someone I
haven't seen in a while and I will have the opportunity to either renew the relationship or perhaps
find some closure in it. There is one particular fellow I see every few months, by happenstance, -
whom I shared a class with fourteen years ago. He
always seems very glad to see me, though he
stands back and doesn't want to shake hands. So
we stop and appreciate seeing each other; a form of
checking in that seems particularly important to
him and which I've learned to enjoy, feeling his
pleasure myself.

A lot of people who share these paths by The Bay
share the urban habits of avoiding eye contact or
keeping an interaction with strangers to a mini-

mum, but walks by the water also attract a dispro-
portionately large number of people who are openly pleased to see others enjoying the scene and the
day. Several times I have met people with whom
I've developed very intimate relationships.

I have also found that it is often easy to strike up a
conversation with someone I've never seen before
and likely will not again. Some of these meetings
can produce a needed boost to my spirits, either
from their good feelings or from a sense of there-
but-for-the-grace-of-god-go-I. And sometimes I
find myself being remarkably candid about the
person's circumstances, delivering to complete
strangers some very powerful advice in comments
on something that they related to me.

Again, it is not about ownership or ego gratifica-
tion. I have had a number of experiences where I
will stop to pet a dog and wind up talking about
important, problems or circumstances in the life of
the person at the other end of the leash. Perhaps it
is because I am a stranger that they open up. I certainly find it easier, at times, to be direct in com-
menting on something they might say, making
connections that I might be hesitant to make with
someone I already know.

Just as I would appreciate the difference between
care-worn thoughts and a clear bolt from the blue,
so have I recognized that the advice I deliver in

these circumstances is untainted by any personal overlay, since I wouldn't know these people or have any motivation for them to act or experience anything in a particular way.

I infer from these experiences that I have been truly useful to these people; that I am providing valuable different information or context for them.

It certainly has happened the other way. I would start talking with someone about his dog, and the conversation would go off in different directions. I might reveal something that I was working with and get a useful new perspective back. Or I might hear a story that offered me a new way to think about a parallel situation in my own life.

(Sidebar: When the allergy season isn't upon me, I have walked through Tennessee Valley to the ocean five days a week. Rarely on weekends because of the increased human traffic, many of whom are children, who don't seem to have other places to bounce and shout.

One Sunday evening, I walked down the Valley just before sundown. I met and began talking to Janey, mostly about on-line computing and spiritual ideas. She mentioned Redfield's book, *The Celestine Prophecy* and talked about synchronicity.

The next day, at a much earlier time, I ran into her again, and again the conversation came around to synchronicity. That's why I got and read the book, and found it significantly informative.)

The people I've encountered – especially during these past three years, and in retrospect for a long time now – have communicated all sorts of information, directly and otherwise, to me and from me. The more open I am – the more relaxed and available – the more information of substance and value comes my way. Sometimes it is particular and important, for instance, a professional contact. And sometimes it is more *scenic*, that is, something illustrative of the scope and complexity of Nature.

Another reason for the walks is that I will frequently see some display of Nature that specifically jogs a metaphoric response. It might be, as mentioned earlier, thinking of the mythic qualities of a snake. Or it might be that I see a flock of shorebirds take off in the same instant, fly off in one direction, veer off in another; looking less like hundreds of birds moving in perfect synchrony than like a single cloud. Depending on the time of day and the angle of the sun, a flock of hundreds of terns can suddenly change direction and literally disappear from sight; until they change direction and catch the sun again.

I think, how do these creatures, with brains smaller than a peanut, manage this outlandish feat of precision flying? And how do they communicate, not only with the other birds in immediate proximity, but with those on the other side of the *cloud*?

(Sidebar: And, for that matter, how do the swallows know when and how to go to San Juan Capistrano on the same day every year? And how do the Monarchs manage to fly the length of the Western Hemisphere and back, with over five generations of butterflies making the trip?)

When I lived with my dog on the beach in Carmel, the tick season would start, run its course, and stop. One day, I'd find the first couple of tickets on her; in three days, I would be finding dozens. At the end of the season, the number would drop back to a couple and then none in just two days. The allergy season starts the same way for me. For the past three years, the sneezing and itchy eyes have started on April thirtieth, and by the second week in June, most of the discomfort is gone.)

Do we need to know how It happens? Perhaps not. It could just be about tiny receivers (in the birds, the ticks and the plants) that respond to the Earth's magnetic Poles and the angle of the sun; not that that facility isn't an extraordinary thing in itself. Can we know what It is? Perhaps not intellectually, but we certainly can see that It happens.

And none of that is the point. The point, at least from my experience and the reason that I am recounting it, is that I saw these shorebirds do their mind-arresting, aerial acrobatics, and it got me to thinking about the wonder of Nature again. The wonder of the same Nature that is in me, mostly unrecognized or understood by my conscious mind. Incredible powers that are either taken for granted or simply overlooked.

Whatever the instigation, it is sights like these that lead us toward discovering that It is in our own lives. Here is how Robert Johnson put it at the end of *Transformation*:

When the dark night begins to lift, one morning there is an unaccountable touch of joy in the air. It is the tiniest trickle of energy, light, and hope, but enough to keep you alive. This is the first contact with the four-dimensional consciousness, and one can begin to live from that source of energy. Something of the subtle inner world becomes your center of gravity: poetry, music, a new perceptiveness when you are jogging, a blossoming of philosophic inquiry, a new religious understanding – something of this world captures you.

And if you'd hold off thinking about this just for a moment or two, here is a third reason why I find it productive to walk amidst Nature. Most of the time I will walk in familiar if beautiful places, and I will find myself involved in a train of thought that can send me along for hundreds of yards at a stretch before I look up and actually *see* the beauty of what's around me.

I wouldn't have the same pleasant time walking through the financial district amidst the cement, glass, honking horns, car fumes, and human crowds. The very fact of being out in Nature, surrounded by the flora and fauna, necessarily colors my experience. The birds are still singing, the flowers still look lovely, the air is still delicious. Even if I am not focused on them, I'm *seeing* and *hearing* them.

And though they don't have my immediate or constant attention, they still affect me, if only on a non-conscious level. As important as are my thoughts, as brilliant as may be a new idea, I am still, as I walk through this glorious garden of subtle sounds, sights, and smells, awash in the nonetheless of Nature.

I couldn't escape It if I wanted. I could easily generate adequate emotional and/or intellectual distraction to mitigate against my experience of the environment – something I might well want to do in the city. But with the natural benefits of being outside on a beautiful day with red-winged blackbirds trilling their concertos, California poppies seeking to redefine orange, and warm, sea-tinged air massaging every exposed pore on my body, the fact is that I don't have to struggle or force anything. Not only can I relax and not have to make an effort to shield myself, I can *come home* to this celebration of Nature.

And in that choice of environment and attitude, I am making a crucial decision in favor of the Self.

Chapter Eleven

The CD-ROM dictionary that came with this word processor defines *mind's eye* as "(1)The inherent mental ability to imagine or remember scenes, and (2) The imagination." Those who don't like the idea of a Larger Reality that invades or influences our own mind will suggest that ideas, imagination, and memory are simply a process of electro-chemical impulses recorded somewhere in the cerebellum. This process, they say, explains the entire panoply of acquisition, storage, and retrieval of information in the human mind.

This description doesn't really expand to cover the explanation for the source of new ideas. But for the moment, let's focus not on where the information comes from but where and how it is displayed.

We all get images in our mind, somewhere behind our eyes, whether they're opened or closed. That is, we can see images in our mind while we are seeing actual objects with our eyes. If you are like me, you see gauzy images, like rear-screen projections, between you and what you are looking at. They appear to me as though they were being displayed on a teleprompter glass.

Do you know the image? When, for example, the president is delivering the State of the Union, you can see squarish glass plates below on either side and in front of the podium; they appear clear when seen head on. But if you get an angled shot, from above and behind, you will see that a script is scrolling slowly up the glass, projected from below by a television monitor. As the president looks out over his audience, delivering his momentous words as though they were a spontaneous transmission from God, in fact, he is merely reading off of electronic cue cards.

This is not unlike the way the mind's eye operates, with the critical exception that the script that appears on our screen is not always one that we have written or want to read.

When we ask ourselves a question, or when we face a situation that calls for information, we project an answer in the mind's eye. A picture, a video, or a series of words appears on that screen inside of our mind. If you think about your mother, you would likely see an image of your mother. If you remember that you are responsible for dinner tonight, you might ask yourself what you'd like to eat, and you might see a salad or pork chops.

Often you will dialogue with, rather than control, these images. Asking about dinner, you might see a picture of a very healthy salad, and argue for the pork chops. Similarly, you might be entertaining a fantasy of an attractive co-worker and suddenly she will get up and walk away; out of your fantasy. Or you might be struggling with the question of how to get the new word processor to print labels the way that you want, and suddenly, you get the idea "Create a table!"

The information can appear as pictures or as words. I sometimes *see* yellow-gold electrical impulses that look like lightning, which almost instantaneously turn into *unseen* thoughts. Curiously, too, I am aware of the content of the impulses before I cognitize them into thought. I actually sense the idea before I translate it into consciousness.

This especially happens when I am writing, but also in every day situations. For instance, I have some errands to run, and I will run a scan of where I am going and the order in which I want to go to the different places. I will know that I have an itinerary in my mind before I actually see images of the road and the stops.

As discussed earlier, this exchange of information, carried on entirely in one's own mind – invisible from the outside but perhaps for a grimace, a look of disappointment, or a broad smile – is a dialogue between two distinctly different voices. I am asking questions, and coming up with answers. Sometimes it's remarkably mundane, as is much of what occupies most of our waking thought, and at other times, it jumps to the edge of new knowledge.

It involves hypothesis and projection, speculation mixed with anticipation – positive and negative – using information that has been stored as fact, together with possibility, plausibility, desire, need, and dread. This forum of the mind's eye is really our own private movie studio where we project plots that extend far beyond a mere choice of entrées or highway exits. It is where we try out ideas about our own life – to see if they will work, to assess risk and return, to assuage guilt, to encourage or abase ourselves, to dampen optimism to prevent action, to infuse ourselves with courage. It is the whole range of human motivation activity, and we are screening our options.

I recall, twelve years ago, driving south on I-5 headed for Desert Hot Springs; it was late and I'd been driving for almost eight hours. I started projecting an image about my checking in at a motel I'd never been to, presenting myself to a clerk I'd never seen; both generic and unidentified. There I was standing at the counter with my wallet open taking out my credit card. And the question I was asking myself as I played out this story in my mind's eye as I was flying down the highway in a ton of steel and glass at 75 miles per hour was, "Who am I going as?"

The very size of the question forced me to slow down. "Who am I going as?" asked how was I presenting myself? But that led immediately to Who am I? Well, I said to myself as I dealt consciously with the question – while another part of my mind spooled too many other and varied thoughts to consider – I was myself who had decided I needed to get away, so I'd gotten in my car and started driving south, thinking maybe I wanted to drive to Northern Mexico. Also, I was a writer. Between consulting gigs, I added.

I realized that my description to myself was as insignificant to myself as I would be insignificant to the clerk at the motel. The real significance to me was that someone – I – was going to decide on what Personality I would be *wearing*. I was going to present myself with certain stereotypical characteristics that would define me to the clerk.

So who did I go as normally? How did that vary from who I would be checking in as that night? What were the circumstances that called for presenting different characteristics – still stereotypical and thus identifiable? And the big one...Who am I going as in my life?

We do it all the time, of course, changing character-istics to fit different situations. Aggressive on the softball base paths but not behind the wheel of the car. Romantic with the wife but not with the daughter. Deferential to the boss but not to the maid. Intelligent to the employee but not to the auto mechanic. Insistent with the son but not with the cop.

A closet full of personalities; we have a file cabinet full of custom-designed outfits that we take out and put on to fit the particular occasion. These presentation packages are like full-featured soft-ware applications that include our comportment, attitude, expectations, humor, and various levels of assertion and obsequiousness. They position us for the people and circumstances that we are to en-counter.

They can be changed or customized in the blink of an eye, but most people try to avoid situations where a radical shift would be required. We are basically uncomfortable with having to tailor our established presentations in any substantial way. That would be like putting ourselves in the close company of a stranger.

We design and implement these presentations based on our presumptions of what other people expect of us, how we think we are supposed to behave, and what quantity and quality of contribution to the interaction we expect to have to generate in order to achieve our projected goals.

Consciously and unconsciously, we make choices in advance and during the engagement, within a range of known parameters. For example, when we go to a party, we will know in advance that the attire will be somewhere between jeans and black-tie, that we'll be bringing a casserole for a pot luck or a bottle of wine in appreciation, and that we are going to have fun or to mingle professionally.

So it is with every waking encounter we have. Of course, we are not usually aware of consciously selecting the particular Personality, of putting it on, or even of having the option. But not only do we do it incessantly, fine-tuning for arrivals and departures of different specific and unknown individuals and circumstances, but we usually preview these Personalties in the mind's eye before hand, to see that they *fit*.

Think of how differently you will behave when you answer the door to a neighbor child selling Girl Scout cookies, a pair (you never see them alone) of Jehovah's Witnesses, a policemen, or Ed McMahon. Think of your behavior with the boy from the mailroom, a colleague, your supervisor, or the chairman of the board.

Who generates these Personalities? Who chooses the appropriate one? How do you define and select the criteria for determining appropriateness? How much flexibility do you think you will need in adapting to a situation? When do you stop fine-tuning and change entirely?

(Sidebar: The phone rang a few minutes ago. I thought I recognized the voice of a friend. We bantered. Then he got off on something about "the dictator of Israel." I knew (1) that it wasn't the person I had thought it was, and (2) that I didn't know who it was. Without changing my tone, I shifted my internal posture; I didn't need to be in the conversation any more, but I didn't feel a need to bail out immediately. Curiosity kept me in another twenty seconds, and then came the opportunity to say "thank-you," to which I added "good night.")

We constantly entertain projections for our every day life. Even in a very restricted existence, the number of thoughts that play out in long-range and on-site projection numbers in the tens of thousands. Most are repetitious, or minor variations on familiar themes of our lives; tweaking as opposed to wholesale alterations. Much of the activity is almost like a personal manservant keeping our lives in order.

How extraordinary it is, for example, to absent-

mindedly drive past the exit you take every morning to go to work. It is not that we don't know how
to remedy the situation or absorb the inconven-
ience, but there was this failure to monitor your
projected path correctly. Perhaps you were
discombobulated because when the day started
you were late getting out of the house. And when
the supervisor caught you, in your mind you ran
through the standard excuses of car trouble and a
sick child, and then remedies like, Sorry and you'll
work later.

But then a thought had presented itself in your
mind – a powerful urge to tell him to Take this job
and.... But that's not like you. Oh; who is it like?
You thought you liked the job? Why did that
thought appear in your mind?

Of course, what is significant, again, about the
mind's eye is less the content but the source. Where
there is a multi-party discussion going on, there
must be different interests generating the different
views and voices. But are they all sourced to the
same origin? Who controls them? Is there a hierarchy? And, not esoterically, which one of them is the
real you?

Chapter Twelve

A few years ago, I realized that I was running a lot of my expectations through the lens of what I then named my Precautionary Mind. This was the voice in me, I discovered, that protected me from the ravages of failure and disappointment by projecting the worst case result to see if I could *live* with it. The plausibility of this worst case, would, by definition, be stretched beyond reason in most cases, but at least I would be inured from horrible consequences.

Actually, I was not. This Precautionary Mind, which had served me valiantly, and probably well, for years, was functioning in my middle age essentially along the lines of its original instructions, which I had likely programmed around the age of four. But what I realized was that it was causing me to experience the feelings of the worst-case failure in advance, whether I would have failed or not. I processed – and to some degree experienced – the disappointment so that I wouldn't be nailed by it later.

This was taking a regrettable toll. I was living with advance worry, not only of failures that I might have to face, but for the many that I wouldn't, since I would often disengage from a particular process before it would come to resolution.

This is not to say that I shouldn't think through things that need consideration when I have the opportunity. But to suffer the consequences of an action that might or might not happen, and in a negative way, before it would actually happen, is an unnecessarily draining, self-abusive process. It is as misguided as celebrating a positive outcome in advance of the reality.

The other primary issue involving this practice of the Precautionary Mind is that it taints the process with an overlay of negative expectation. Having already viewed the worst case result and prepared for it by suffering the failure in advance, I had actually invested in the outcome, and could, in fact, have poisoned the proverbial well. And we all know people who are actually disappointed when things turn out better than they expected.

Though I saw this pattern of behavior years earlier, I found it to be something not easily shed. The more I lean forward with hopes and worries, the more I find myself off balance. More than a decade

ago, I came up with the suggestion to my Precautionary Mind – said by others many times in different ways over the millennia – *Don't let expectations
temper aspirations.* Sound advice; would that I
would take it.

My father, a noted psychoanalyst, informed me
more than once that it didn't matter so much what
thoughts I might have as what I did with them. On
the surface, this isn't unreasonable. Strong *feelings*
of hostility translated into violent action, like amo-
rous thoughts enacted toward a disinterested part-
y, can have unwanted consequences.

But what you think *is* important – and yes, what
you do or don't do with the thoughts – but also the
very fact of the thoughts. Because as bizarre
thoughts as you may have – like dreams of having
sex with your mother – they are not really about
the images but they are metaphors. So, addressing
my father's point, Right, I didn't have sex with my
mother, or want to, but I don't have to let it go
there. I can examine the archetypal issues that I
find in the imagery; about maternal versus oedipal
love, for example.

A second consideration about bizarre thoughts is
that they may simply be misinterpreted. If the left
lobe translates the imagery that comes through the
right lobe, it may be that the left lobe doesn't have
the vocabulary to make the translation of some-

thing unknown, and it fastens onto the closest definition it can find. Like an automatic spell checker.
The more limited the vocabulary – by experience,
awareness, and attitude – the less open one is going
to be to alternatives in particular and the larger
picture in general.

(Sidebar: We engage in the same process sometimes when listening to a person who is speaking
in an accent or in a voice too low to be clear. We
will wait to pick up words at the end of a sentence
or statement that will provide clues and context
that we might – correctly or incorrectly – extrapo-
late to infer the overall meaning.)

This concept needs more discussion, but first an
introduction to a corollary process to the Precautionary Mind – what I refer to as the Retributive
Mind. I first saw it when I was sitting outside of a
friend's office, waiting for him to get free. He was
fifteen minutes late, and I found myself on the
verge of getting annoyed.

Suddenly I saw that I was, in fact, watching myself
in the process of deciding that I should be annoyed.
In point of fact, I didn't feel annoyed; I wasn't in a
hurry, and he knew that I was outside, so whatever
he was doing needed his attention. Further, I realized that he knew that I would know that.

I knew in that moment that I could still tell myself

that I felt slighted, and that I could put on that attitude of negativity, justifiably – he was keeping me waiting, after all – but that it would be a construct made up entirely out of concept and not out of my true feelings or thoughts.

The Retributive Mind, which will need more exploration at another time, is a structure for judging. It keeps the balance sheet for all aspects of my life. Am I doing enough in this relationship? Am I giving away too much in another? Am I being treated with appropriate respect, warmth, affection? My Retributive Mind keeps score, deciding who is in favor and who isn't, and whether or not I am keeping up my end of the bargain.

What is important to note here is that the Retributive and Precautionary Minds (1) operate from a primitive formation, (2) they start from an emotional, fight-flight foundation, (3) they define the intellectual posture that will color new and emergent thoughts, and (4) they are very powerful, difficult to remove, tame, or re-train.

These primal aspects of the Personality are important because they wield so much influence and because they so dominate the mind. As George Leonard noted frequently in his lectures, a fundamental rule of mind-body connection is that energy follows attention. When you are paying attention to what you are doing or where you are going, you are less likely to slip up. Whether it is walking down a rocky slope or pouring a can of frozen lemonade into a small-necked bottle, the more attentive I am to what I am doing, the less likely I am to have a spill.

Concomitantly, the less of an overlay – Precautionary or Retributive (and there are others) – that I have when I encounter a situation, the more directly and effectively I am going to meet it. Without the baggage of preconception – intellectual or tonal (mood) – the more cleanly I am going to engage whatever comes my way.

Obviously, my mood is going to color how I greet the day, or any individual who may come along during it. If my mind is soaring with a grand new idea, traffic is less likely to be an annoyance. If I've just gotten turned down on a business proposal, that old lady in front of me had better move her boat out of my lane.

I find that my emotions create an overlay of my left brain (and Personality), so that if I am feeling negative, the ideas and the people I think about, I think about negatively. In a good mood, I approach people and things more hopefully. It used to be that I would allow my Personality to operate in a negative state, thinking that it offered some benefit to me, e.g., going deeper into my emotional self and venting ill feelings. But I no longer believe that to be the case, so when I feel that negativity, I make every effort not to operate in that mood, or to reduce my contact with people, projects, and ideas.

Moods are not intuitive feelings, but are an emotional state engendered by the thinking side. Intuition, unadulterated, is clear information that comes through in a non-sensate feeling way. Our misinterpretation of that feeling is what puts us in a particular mood. Any time you have a feeling that pushes you toward an attitude, stop yourself as quickly as you can. Quiet your mind, and allow the feeling to wash through you without judgment.

Usually, we are triggered by the onset of certain feelings to go into a mental posture based on habit, inculcated in our very first years. The sooner we can interrupt this process of transforming from feeling to mood, the easier it is to get underneath our programmed response, and to experience the intuitive information cleanly. Surprisingly, I've discovered, most intuitive feelings that result in bad moods are actually very nurturing, now that I don't let my thinking side interpret them.

The more often I have made the effort not to succumb to this old pattern, the more it has become possible to intervene before unwarranted and/or undesirable behavior is manifested through that negative overlay. It has been an exercise in untying myself from a early-formed behavior pattern that doesn't serve me, in concept or in fact. And as I have practiced this intervention, successfully, the more time I have to stop the process, and the less tendency I have to go into a mood.

This has been of critical importance to me because, as has been observed by a lot of people who have known me, I've had a lot of anger inside. And not only does it mean that I don't get into a lousy mood, as easily or as often, but it concomitantly demonstrates my capacity to work in restructuring my Personality. By not getting angry when I don't have to, or at least as often, I demonstrate a greater flexibility in responding to situations.

(Sidebar: One key example for me occurred many years ago when I lived in a small upper-middle class apartment building in New York City. I heard some shouting in the hallway a couple of floors below. When I went to investigate, I discovered that a woman was being angrily berated by her drug addict son who had climbed in her window. When I came onto the scene, he started screaming at me. Rather than getting defensive, which is what I *normally* would have done, I didn't take his attack personally. Instead, I told him calmly that my mother was sick upstairs and was having trouble sleeping. It wasn't true, but it didn't matter. He calmed down, apologized, and soon left.)

This process of going into the feeling side of my

mind is particularly difficult for a modern Western man, because over the past three hundred years of Cartesian beliefs, we have been instructed to live in the sensate and intellectual world. Feelings showed weakness; that was where women lived.

Part of what this transformation is about is the recognition of the limitations of the thought-dominated male mind. Intuition is too powerful a tool to ignore, or to undervalue. Men who are more intuitive are more creative, and, in most ventures, more successful.

The flip side is that the women who have joined the male world and, following suit (sic), e.g., sublimated their intuitive, have had a far unhappier time of it. Suicide, heart disease, alcoholism, broken relationships, and other *badges* of the male industrial society have increased dramatically among the women who have tried to compete using a masculine overlay and constraining their feminine instincts.

When people talk about confronting their dark side, they're really talking about reconciling with their natural, feeling side; about reincorporating their intuition. But there has been so much opprobrium about the non-sense side of our beings that we view such an exploration as a failure, or weakness, rather than seeing it for what it really is – a joining with our non-intellectual side. Rather than it being a confrontation, it is actually a unification, a discovery of the fullness of our being.

Calling it the dark side had negative connotations for me, but that view was radically dispelled when I realized that it was only darkness to the senses. That my senses couldn't perceive the non-sensate intuitive – by definition – meant only that it would be unilluminated, and hence dark. But once I started the exploration, not only could there be no objection from the senses, but from the intuitive came a sense of absolute joy.

Going into the dark side, into the intuitive, is not about facing the bad part of a person, but enjoining the truth. The intuitive is another medium of information from the pre-Personality source...the Spirit. The reason for the negative description of this process is that the Personality, as a matter of its own preservation, doesn't want the intuitive to be discovered as another, more direct and substantial source of information, feelings, and direction.

The more you understand that the struggle in the mind is the Personality fighting to maintain dominance, thinking it means survival, the easier it is to dialogue about a new role for the Personality. Beyond an issue of enlightenment, more than a matter of choice, it is the formulation of new policy for the whole human being, based on a re-assessment of (1) where you are, (2) how you got here, (3) where you are going, and (4) how you will get there.

You will need an interface with Other as long as you are drawing a breath, so there will always be a need for the Personality. You need to know this so that the Personality isn't threatened with extinction, which is what the radical transformation may look like at times.

In essence, the reconstitution of the Personality means that its role shifts from defending the Self to Other, to truly and fully representing the interests of the Self. Once the new direction is understood, it can be incorporated. The work is easier, and much more rewarding. Immediately.

Chapter Thirteen

In his book *The Origin of Consciousness in the Breakdown of the Bicameral Mind*, Julian Jaynes described two ways of thinking about ourselves. One is the analogue I, which is life from our individual point of view. The other is the metaphor me, which is a view of our Self in life from the outside.

In a way, the Precautionary Mind represents the former individual-as-subject while the Retributive Mind refers to the individual-as-object perspective. In both cases, the issue is the positioning of our Personality in the social structure.

Indeed, most of our thinking has to do more with a cost-benefit analysis of our positioning of the our Personality in the group than in who our Self is and what is really best for us. How we relate to our surroundings is our dominant concern. Consider that the second question that we are asked when we meet someone for the first time (after our name) is What do you do?, i.e., what is your work, how do you make your money, what is your role in society?

Society defines our value by how we make our money.

We define our own value by how we spend it.

Other critical factors that determine our position in society are personal appearance – consider the size and scope of the fashion and cosmetics industries – how we live, what kind of things we own, and what kind of car we drive. These are primary issues in our lives, often more important in the eyes of society than how we raise our children or conduct ourselves in business.

How we are viewed by society is a pervasive concern. When I was traveling on business in the Seventies, I would frequently be dining alone. Rarely would I sit without writing somewhat ostentatiously in my notebook; it said that I was deliberately alone, as opposed to being shunned, or lonely.

A year or so ago, I walked out of the post office and headed off toward my car. Suddenly I stopped when I realized that I had parked my car in another part of the lot. Instead of just changing direction, I looked down at my watch, as though I was considering the hour and decided I had the time to alter my plans.

It was an extraordinary act. It presumed that (1) someone was watching me, and (2) they cared what I was doing and where I was going. It wasn't paranoia, it was simply the desire to be presenting myself – performing my role in society – perfectly; and not making mistakes; like forgetting where I had parked my car. This desire to be upright was very deeply ingrained. In fact, at the time of the incident, I would have been embarrassed to re-count the story.

Which word, embarrassment, underscores this process of seeking approval. Embarrassment, after all, is about being *caught* by someone doing something that otherwise we wouldn't find objection-able, e.g., picking one's nose. Russell Baker noted in a column years ago that many people will lie if they are awakened by a phone call and asked if they had been sleeping. As if taking a nap was a bad thing; as if we should always be awake and participating.

Society is saturated with reminders about staying in line, e.g., Don't call attention to yourself and Don't rock the boat. Standing out from the crowd is a risky proposition. There are rewards, to be sure, but there are also dangers. And rarely do we recog-nize and appreciate those pioneers who are the cutting edge, the paint on the prow of the ice-breaker, who lead us to new understandings of who we are and how we are to re-assemble our-selves together in a new way.

Approval is the core to keeping ourselves in line. An outgrowth of the punishment-reward system and the go along-get along social structure, approval is our gyroscope, for as long as it serves us, and then some. In the family, in school, at work, we learn to toe the line because the consequences of not – a spanking, a bad report card, and a pink slip – are worse than the cost of compliance.

For most of us.

Most of the time.

So far.

But the conflicts are growing, in number and in importance, between anachronistic concepts of obeisance and new realities. There is a wonderful parable in the Grace Notes section on Zen Buddhism in Phillip Novak's *The World's Wisdom* called "Carry the Girl." It's the story of two monks who come to the bank of a river and discover a girl in her finery who can't cross the shallow river. Even though it is "wrong" to touch a young woman, one of the monks carries her across the river on her back and deposits her dry on the other bank. Later, the other monk is critical of the one for having touched the woman. Said the monk, "I set her down by the river. But; you are still carrying her."

readily penetrable to our learning-limited vision. It has been easy to warn of dangers in the un-visible. Consider all of the odium associated with the word black, e.g., black heart, blackball, black hand, blackguard, black cat, to name a few.

Society is safe if we don't look into the darkness, and as long as we are comfortable with society, we will remain blind to the apple of knowledge and the greater truth. Our indoctrination against the knowing more has been going on for so long that even when society isn't meeting our needs, we are not likely to explore the darkness very quickly; certainly not without significant additional incentive.

The basic compact of contemporary society is that people who work hard and obey the rules will have security and the opportunity to advance. But the notion of security is false. Our Social Security system – in fact and as a metaphor – is a sham. The current surplus in payments has been going to reduce the U.S. deficit while our *trust* fund is being filled with unredeemable IOU's. Our prisons don't work, nor do our schools. The rich are getting richer and the poor poorer. There is a dangerous, declining sense of community. And with our institutions losing their cachet, a growing number of people are being forced back on themselves rather than upholding society.

Is There a Why?

Most people struggle to remain part of the system and will move, change jobs, and in small but often important ways alter their behavior to remain members, in their own as well as in their public minds. Increasingly, however, it's getting tougher to *hang in there*. People are feeling pulled further away from their own instincts or intuition. This is why stress is such a big factor in our society; why so many people are killing themselves with opioids, alcohol, tobacco, and overeating; why so many millions of our colleagues, friends, and family are taking anti-depressants.

We are a very different culture from who we were in the Sixties, and it is tearing us apart; as a society and as individuals. The Sixties were about participation and hope; it was a time of true community, when we declared the beginning of the end of war, gender bias, and race discrimination.

The people in charge, those who had something to lose in a change from the status quo, refused to let go and they have co-opted as many of they needed and could afford to maintain their superior position. The top income tax rate dropped from over 94% to 34%. The cream of the middle class was given a ticket – albeit temporary – to a share of the pie. The top one percent of the people doubled their wealth.

Where did the money come from? The future. The

people in charge took out a $5 trillion loan which we now call the national debt, which has climbed to $22 trillion today, and is headed for $34 trillion in the next decade...equal to the nation's GDP.

What will happen when there is no work for the mass of the unskilled, when jobs are shifted out of the country or taken over by robots? What will what's left of the middle class – and the poor – do to put food on the table?

Is it just a coincidence that the rise in individual Self-exploration comes about with a decline in social affinity; that the social Personality is jeopardized by withdrawal of the individual participants while the individual Personality is in jeopardy from a similar re-assertion by the Self? Is it not plausible that the institutions we created to support the Industrial Age don't serve us in the post-Industrial Age, and that we are shedding like dead skin the long-held presumptions that held our society together?

Consider that the internet is in the process of making all of the world's information available to everyone, any time and any place. The collective conscious of the planet will be accessible through every computer keyboard and smartphone. Our success – our survival – will be determined by what information we select, and what we do with it.

Buckminster Fuller said he thought the Earth could sustain a billion people. Whether or not his figure is precisely or even close to accurate, we do know that the planet is vastly over-populated. Now over seven billion, we are grossly over-weight as a species, and we will either have to trim our numbers intentionally – not by murder but by birth control and attrition – or we will run out of resources and the re-balancing process will occur anyway.

The crumbling of our foundations, the massive debt, global proliferation of weapons of mass destruction among unstable governments and smaller entities, a rise in zealotry and terrorism – we are a planet ripe for change. And if indeed we are witnessing as it appears a transformation on a global level, then we should not be surprised at a change of similar scope taking place in the individual.

A significant percentage of our fellow citizens have responded to the chaos by looking inward. It was a process that started in the Sixties and got seriously underway in the Seventies – *The Me Decade* – though it was widely viewed as narcissism.

Perhaps this is a natural, inter/national process. The United States, the global synthesis of East and West, was founded on the principles of rights and opportunity. Alexis De Tocqueville, the Frenchman who wrote *Democracy in America* in 1835 after extensive travels in the young and newly-forming

Chapter Fourteen

The confusion about, and concomitant fear of, the dark side is pervasive in our culture. The first three *Star Wars* films (I didn't see the others) were about the dialectic of *The Force* on the one hand and *The Dark Side* on the other. Darth Vader and the Emperor were dressed in black; after his redemption, and death, Vader wore white.

But the dark side is not actually about evil and its enticements. Rather, this image is fostered by society's need to keep people away from their own truth. The fact is that the more we discover the truth about our own greater power as individuals – when we are less shackled to the social order – the more we contribute to the shredding of the anachronistic knots in the social fabric.

Of course society, in its desire to preserve itself, would discourage our looking into the darkness where we would discover our true power, and, consequently, invest in ourselves as individuals instead of putting the group first. Society has been able to foster this lie because the darkness is not country, observed that this is a nation of strong individualism. American readers took it as a compliment, but Europeans had a different view: they saw a danger of fragmentation to the social order.

But maybe, in this age of holding paradox, there is some practical purpose to being both a nation and still-pioneering individuals. Perhaps we have a greater than obvious capacity to eschew social constraints and to manage for ourselves. Maybe this characteristic is a part of our national psyche that has brought us to trail-blaze from amber waves of grain to amber waves of light, or whatever comprises that next stage beyond the intellectually sensate.

Chapter Fifteen

For those ready to explore further, there is probably much in their own experience that they can look to as evidence that they have already had – and are currently in the midst of – significant change in their lives. Otherwise, you probably wouldn't have read this far. Such change might involve a feeling of dis-ease with society at large, an inability to make small talk, and finding what you thought was important – work, relationships, hobbies, ideas – to mean less.

Unfortunately, at least for many on the cutting edge of this transformation, the only route to higher consciousness requires leaving a lot behind; the pain, depending on how much there is to uproot and how deep the roots go, can be quite a cost.

To reach a higher level of consciousness means re-examining – and often eliminating – basic pre-sumptions about how things work, and what is our role in it all. To shift those foundations means digging very deep, like a dentist going under the gums, to scrape out the last vestiges of antiquated Personality; the base macros (behavioral patterns) of perception and response; the final shreds of control.

But once you abandon everything, even hope, and you find yourself still breathing, you come to realize that there is indeed a point to your life, even though you may not know what it is. And it is there for you to realize it. You wouldn't have to go through this hell, as others have liberally described it, if there weren't some purpose. Part of the new physics is that nothing is wasted. If you weren't important to establishing a new sense of Self – as an individual and as a co-creator of the next social structure – then you wouldn't have had to go (put yourself) through the unlearning and the new *training*.

Maybe it will be easier for those who follow, but in the first wave it seems to require deep spiritual redefining of the meaning and value of this life. I never really considered suicide as an option, but I thought about it; the pain of despair would get that intense. Does someone have to go to these depths, to rip out the last glimmer of identity – that's what it feels like – in order to learn what one needs to know?

One purpose of writing this book is to mitigate

some of the pain caused by the unknowing. But it is a shallow salve. As it is put in the Legend of Buddha's Life, *A man must take medicine to be cured; the mere sight of the physician is not enough.*

What is required is looking back into the energy stream that is generating the Personality. This is like turning a balloon inside out, while it has air in it. With the balloon itself making the decision.

But since the Spirit comes into the individual as Self, and since the Self creates the Personality as an interface with the rest of the world, then for a person (the Personality) to decide to look back toward Self means taking an enormous risk that will, if he goes through with the process, mean the functional demise – at least a major restructuring – of the "person" making the decision.

That's an iffy step for an Armani-clad, Beamer-driving, cool young thing pulling down a seven-figure salary. And for the single mother supporting her children working two jobs. The most likely candidates will be those people who have been successful enough that they can manage to keep things together while they explore the core issues of their lives, but not so successful that they want to stay with the program.

It may be the first time, in fact, that a r/evolutionary step of any magnitude has been perpetrated by a segment of the population that is otherwise comfortable. Normally it would be the masses against the elite, or one group of elite toppling another.

Another unique characteristic of this transformation is that it is being conducted as a withdrawal of participation, rather than an act to overthrow and replace the existing structure and/or command with another.

The third, and most powerful element of the shift, is that the conversion is not a group process. The movement is one of people changing direction individually; like people getting up in the middle of a performance and departing en masse without prior agreement. What will make it look like a movement is the relative simultaneity of reaching a certain level of awareness. Like those shorebirds taking off together.

The signs of radical change abound. There are a also some good clues about what directions individuals can take in their own lives to facilitate the process. Joseph Campbell gave the simplest instruction: *Follow your bliss.* If you have no other reference point, just determining your bliss is a good starting point. It is advice that most people say that they are too busy to follow.

A second *exercise* is to relax and get out into Nature

more. It doesn't have to take significant effort, but the more time you spend away from machines, electricity, and the emotional static generated by others, the quieter you can get your own mind. And consequently, the easier it is to generate a clear and productive internal dialogue.

Ueshiba Morihei, the founder of *aikido*, a 20th century martial art, said that you could never learn a technique for every situation, only how to respond and in the moment. It wasn't that he had learned every possible move, only how to process so quickly that to the unpracticed eye, it looked as though he was reacting spontaneously. Because in aikido, as in every activity, the purpose of training is to tune the human mind to operate the human body without deliberation.

Watch a stenographer; she doesn't have to be cognitive of what she is typing to rattle out over a hundred words a minute. Or on the wider keyboard, the accomplished pianist doesn't think "C-major...A-flat...B-minor"; the notes fly off the sheet music and instigate a series of coordinated eye-hand movements that turn out to be Chopin. And if LeBron James thought for a fraction of a second about lift, velocity and torque, he wouldn't be scoring thirty points in a game.

Training brings increased fluidity of movement through practice, but it is the ability to conduct the process – without thinking deliberately about what you are doing – that defines success, and pleasure. When you take the editor out of the process – when you give up control and go with the flow – you get out of your own way. It is the practice of eliminating middle-management from the decision-making.

Sports is a good arena to see how the mind is able to channel the flow of information away from the cognitive mind. There are familiar expressions that underscore the qualities of top athletes, e.g., He became one with the ball. Top football quarterbacks talk about everything suddenly moving in slow motion; that there was all the time in the world to find a receiver and throw the pass.

I was never a real athlete, but in my thirties I got into playing pick-up softball on Sunday afternoons. It wasn't a very serious game, but playing every weekend got me into shape and I enjoyed the feeling of playing well. As every player knows, hitting the ball with the sweet spot of the bat (or the tennis racket or golf club) provides a momentary feeling of perfection. Even if the ball is caught.

I remember how good it felt to side-arm a long throw from behind third base to first, feeling the purposefulness in my shoulder, elbow, wrist, waist, and legs as I watched the ball arc cross the diamond. And in one particular instant, making a tag

play at second base on a throw from left field without a shred of thought passing through my conscious mind.

I have felt the same peaceful exhilaration driving a
stretch of road by Nicasio Reservoir in western
Marin County. It is an empty, two lane highway,
slightly banked on a long curve. And when I drive
it at around seventy miles an hour, there is a com-
bination of speed and centrifugal force that makes
my body feel deliciously in tune; that massaging,
tingling sensation of well-applied power.

Later, when I learned to fly in Redding, I would
practice my landings. On one occasion, I felt as
though I was wearing the plane.

That internal sweet spot of personal perfection;
performing without thinking; being one with the
Other. It is the same exquisite rhythm that dancers
find. And lovers.

Chapter Sixteen

John Donne's poetic view of death has survived, if that is the right word, now almost four centuries:

No man is an island,
Entire of itself,
Every man is a piece of the continent,
A part of the main.
If a clod be washed away by the sea,
Europe is the less.
As well as if a promontory were.
As well as if a manor of thy friend's
Or of thine own were:
Any man's death diminishes me,
Because I am involved in mankind,
And therefore never send to know for whom the bell
tolls;
It tolls for thee.

It has occurred to me that there would be less of a sense of horror and loss if we better understood the role of death in our world. I'm not talking about the Holocaust, Pol Pot's slaughter of his people, and the myriad wars over the last thirteen millennia. Or the people killed in accidents or by criminals; or those who die prematurely from insidious diseases.

I refer to the end of life process that removes individuals for society's rolls. What if we saw people shuffling off this mortal coil *naturally* simply as actors who dematerialized and moved to another stage of being? That would reduce a considerable amount of pain and sorrow, unnecessary suffering by both the departing person and those who will miss them.

I don't know what happens when a person dies. Who does? I think there is some form of recycling of the Spirit, though I don't know (1) how it works, (2) if we come back right away, (3) if we choose our parents, or (4) if it involves an evolutionary growth process of individuals. My sense is that our Spirit – that which makes us a unique container of the Self – accumulates experience/knowingness, and progresses from one lifetime to the next.

In Tibet, young children who are thought to be incarnated lamas have picked out from an array of objects that were part of their supposed previous life. That may also explain why we meet some young people who seem to be old souls.

Is There a Why?

So if in fact we are all of the same Spirit, recycling through a series of lives, then there is nothing lost, nothing to mourn; it is a stage direction.

*   *   *   *   *

Many years ago, I had an image play out in broad daylight in my mind's eye, which I think reflects the birth-death-rebirth cycle. I was training with Wendy Palmer, who was also my aikido instructor, working in the *dojo* of Aikido of Tamalpais on some practices involving intuition.

I remember clearly that it was cold that day, and Wendy and I were sitting on the mat in a patch of sunlight near a window. In the first exercise, she asked me to close my eyes and clear my mind. Then after a few minutes of focusing on my breathing, she asked me to tell her of the first image that came to mind. It was, and I can see it vividly today, a beautiful, open, black rose, positioned alone at the bottom of a sky-blue backdrop.

I asked Wendy what she had been thinking about. A friend of hers, she said, who was dying of cancer. I had never seen a black rose before, in fact or as an image; nor have I since.

We moved on to another exercise. We walked at an even pace in a large oval around the mat. Holding gently onto Wendy's sleeve while we walked, I closed my eyes and cleared my mind. As we walk-

ed, an extraordinary scene displayed itself in my
mind's eye. I recounted it to Wendy as we walked.
Here is how I wrote about it a few years later:

*I am walking along a beam of yellow golden light; it
leads ahead of me like a pathway, but when I look down,
it's just a beam. And I'm not walking, because I don't
have a real body. I feel ethereal. My presence is very
strong, but I don't see a form.*

*The beam is in the middle of a beautiful day-sky of
white-yellow light; not glaring, but bright, soft in a way
that I don't have to squint. And I can see stars or spar-
kles of some sort, golden and white, twinkling about.
And there are rainbows flowing through the distant
background.*

*I am "walking" along this beam toward something small
and dark, a round opening. It grows larger as I near it,
and I can see that it is like the opening of a tunnel. As I
get closer, I can see that it is a portal onto a realm of
darkness. There are very few stars in that darkness; it is
like nighttime.*

*[Now I have a body.] I am standing within the portal,
my feet lightly braced on the bottom of what appears to
be a circle. My arms stretch out to a relaxed distance as
my hands hold the top of the ring. I'm standing in the
ring, half in the light and half in the darkness.*

*Wendy asks if I am going to enter the darkness. I say I
don't know how. She asks, What happens if you just let*

go? Which I do, and I fall, not down but weightlessly into the darkness; in a somewhat fetal crouch.

Where did these images come from? I had never seen or imagined anything like that in my life. Was the yellow-golden light the realm of Spirit (or heaven)? Was my trip from the light at the end of the tunnel into human life?

My interpretation of this imagery was that it was my Spirit coming into form; my birth, if you will, into the physical realm. I remember feeling some sense of uncertainty about going into the darkness, but it was coupled with a sense of purpose and inevitability. Still, I felt as though I was *leaving home*.

*   *   *   *   *

I think the Spirit cycles through the form and consciousness of human beings as part of a large-scale evolutionary process. Like the tides using waves. Though to what purpose, other than some kind of progressive unfoldment, I don't know.

I don't know that we are capable of knowing. Or, certainly and obviously, that we need to know.

And I think that just as the human being is a mind-bogglingly complex Self-organizing system – the operation of being a person – so is the Spirit a unique entity that needs to reach a certain level of accomplishment or attainment before it moves up to the next stage. And as the Self uses the individual human being, the Spirit uses the human species (and the rest of life on Earth as a support structure) to manifest and evolve its growth.

This means that all of us are part of the Spirit, which should hardly seem a surprise since oneness with the deity – this belief in the godhood in each of us – is the core principle of most of the world's religions. We all share the same source and the same ultimate direction, each playing unique roles in this mutual growth process. We are inevitably to reach some point of critical mass and the next level will be attained.

How many people will it take to trigger and/or reach that critical mass? Millions probably, but as noted before, they will be co-leaders rather than followers. Those waiting for the second coming of a single leader are unlikely to be part of the vanguard.

Metaphorically, it may be like the story of the hundredth monkey. As I recall it, there was a group of monkeys living on an island off of Japan. The monkeys ate sweet potatoes that they dug out of the sand. One day, one monkey washed the sand off of his sweet potato in the water. The next day, they all did.

Or something like that. Maybe it wasn't the next

day, and maybe it took a while for all of the other monkeys to get on board. Oh, and there is some question about veracity of the story, but so what? If it's only a metaphor, the concept is certainly clear.

It is like the first amphibian, but there is a difference. While the lead monkey's behavior may have been the result of evolution of the individual, the response of the others was obviously not a biological jump, but the result of a cognitized visual communication. There was the demonstration of a new behavior, and a consequent and quick decision by the mass to follow.

Watching what happens to some stocks as the result of a hiccup in the news, it's not difficult to imagine that, provided the right information is supplied, in relatively short period of time – perhaps just a few years – tens millions of people could receive that information and act on it. They would learn of the path to a higher level of consciousness, and they would choose to put themselves on it.

I not only think that's how a transformative shift could be instigated or fueled, I think it's a far more likely scenario than a offspring of a god returning to walk on water. And now with the Internet mostly ubiquitous, a spark could produce a lot of light.

To repeat, where the metaphors of the hundredth

monkey and the stock swings are incomplete is that while the information may be made available immediately and to many, it is what can be done with that information that will matter. It won't be enough to read and say Ah-hah. It requires not mimicry but the personal restructuring of perception, and the shifting from social followership to individual re-creation.

Chapter Seventeen

What does intuition tap into? Most of us have intuited information that we know we never knew before. Where do we go for it? How do we get there, more often and deliberately?

Perhaps the answers to these questions, at least for the time being are beyond us. But the questions aren't, and the more we ask them, the closer we get to discovering their answers. It may be that we can only sense the correct direction, but that should be enough. After all, we can't hear light or see sound.

What if every possible bit of information in the universe were truly accessible to us, immediately, and all the time; probably in some sort of holographic form? It might look like a giant wedge of overwhelmingly brilliant light, with the outer side reaching to infinity, and the infinitely tiny point beaming into our own consciousness. (Into our right lobe, as the receiver.)

What decides what information to select? How

clear is the selection process? And how deliberate? Who decides what gets through, when you're awake and when you're asleep? In terms of imagination and creativity, is there any correlation with different levels of consciousness, for instance, people who remember their dreams easily and who deny dreaming altogether?

The left lobe – the editor, the translator – defines how information is interpreted, and with the overarching Personality, determines just how much information shall be cognitized. We are aware of our thoughts, and we are aware of thoughts that we do not, can not, and will not entertain consciously. And even though we won't consider them, or even *know* what they are or are specifically about, we are nonetheless aware of having them.

Northrop Frye, the Canadian literary critic, had an interesting take on the trail of words from thoughts:

It is clear that all verbal structures with meaning are verbal imitations of that elusive psychological and physiological process known as thought, a process stumbling through emotional entanglements, sudden irrational convictions, involuntary gleams of insight, rationalized prejudices, and blocks of panic and inertia, finally to reach a completely incommunicable intuition"

Let's back up for a broader view. To maintain its authority and control, the Personality requires that the perception and presentation of the individual remain relatively consistent. After all, if a person changed his Personality all of the time, there would be no consistent relationship to Other, and hence no need for the Personality. A person could not to relate to life without a basic outline of a personality; without at least some parameters, there would be no definition of the person.

In order then for a person to function, some framework of a Personality must be defined, and a key part of this process is the selection of the information that is allowed to past from the infinite at the gateway of the right lobe into the operating center of the left lobe. This necessarily limits – in terms of both quantity and type – what will be perceived. All of the other information is closed off by the sphincter-like *muscle* controlling the flow to the left lobe.

When we're awake.

Most of the time.

Jaynes wrote in *The Origin of Consciousness...* that it seems impossible for a person to hang out only in one lobe for more than two to four minutes at a time. As hard as we might try to concentrate on something specific, our mind will eventually flip from the left to the right lobe and break the concentration with something different. By the same token, as hard as we might work to keep our mind open to a stream of consciousness, inevitably the left lobe will seize on something *solid* and ponder it.

The foundation of meditation is to pre-occupy the left lobe or cognitive mind until the right lobe or pre-cognitive mind pops in with a thought. Of course, even though a new thought may appear, it will still be interpreted by the Personality-controlled left lobe, which will usually compromise the Spirit-purity of the communication, or at least taint it, to endorse the Personality's perspective.

To protect its position, the Personality creates a template of interpretation that allows certain information and imagery to come into consciousness. The Personality will do some extraordinary twisting of the input. More commonly, think of how some people simply *hear only what they want to hear.*

Recognizing, then, that the Personality is interpreting all of the information that comes to consciousness while we are awake, the challenge is to reduce the amount of interpretive oversight, and to open as clear a channel to the source of ideas and intuition as we can. This is the simple purpose of meditation, of course, but must also be the path in conscious life.

Not knowing what is the source of intuition or how

to get there, at least we can recognize when we are not tapping into it, and then try to shift from there. The first step is to become aware of our perceiving.

While I was driving this morning, I realized that if I focused on the car in front of me, I would see that it was being driven more slowly than it needed to be. However, when I softened my gaze and pulled my focus back, suddenly I realized that I wasn't thinking, or concerned, about the speed of the other car.

Bringing my attention back from the further to the nearer point of reference – from the car in front to my own car – allowed me to disengage from the more specific perspective that involved where I was going in the longer term and the limitations thereof caused by the slower car. Instead, I was able to draw in my boundaries of engagement, to be more *in the moment*, and to no longer be bothered by the inconsiderate yahoo who couldn't find the accelerator.

This is an example of being able to see without looking. Like a runner who is moving so fast that he gets tears in his eyes, the only way he can see is if he slows down. Or driving down a road looking for an address; if you are driving too fast, you can't see the numbers on the houses. Simply by slowing down, or drawing in your perspective, you reduce the volume of information you're engaging, and you can assimilate it more effectively.

And this, I believe, is the path to *seeing* higher consciousness. A number of people suggest that higher consciousness exists in another dimension, which would explain why we can't pick it up with our senses. That kind of talk elicits a lot of *woo-woo* comments from scoffers, but perhaps not fairly.

Our society seems max'd out on three dimensions. The first is existence, represented by a dot.

Looking at that dot another way, it might be the end of a two-dimensional line.

And that line could be the edge of a three-dimensional item, such as a box.

But let's expand our thinking about dimensions. For instance, What is in that box – air, feathers, gold – defines a fourth dimension: density.

A perfectly reasonable fifth dimension would define how long the box has been in existence: duration.

This might seem a bit esoteric, but what we know about the box, its shape, its size, what is in it, and for how long it has been here comprises the sixth dimension: perception.

And not to go too overboard, perhaps there is a seventh dimension where everything that we can't think of related to the box exists. Just because we can't (yet) conceive of it doesn't mean that it doesn't exist. In fact, the idea of another dimension makes sense, defining what is otherwise unknowable or unexplainable. Such information could include the maker of the box, for instance, who filled it, and who owns it.

I say *yet* because I think we are moving toward a concrete perception of this higher reality. Indeed, I think we sometimes glimpse it, but not having an intellectual understanding of what it is, we aren't able to fully perceive it.

This might be similar to the experience of being able to see something out of the corner of our eye but not when we look directly at it. Or that it is possible to see the stars in the sky during the middle of a sunny day, if we stand at the bottom of a well. In both of these cases, it is merely an ocular overload that inhibits us from seeing what is otherwise visible.

These examples prove exception to the pro-sensory belief that Seeing is believing. Another example of the exception-able nature of our sensory ability is when something tastes different from how we would expect it to from the way it smells. Our senses, while exalted in our mechanistic society, are truly limited.

It may also be – indeed, it is likely – that we are still evolving to the point where we will be able to perceive more. In the end of *Transformation*, Robert Johnson notes that our physical senses have continued to develop over the past couple of millennia. The color blue, for example, isn't found in literature as recently as two thousand years ago. And harmony, as opposed to melody, only came into the musical lexicon in the 15th or 16th century.

Another reason why we may not be able to perceive something that we would infer to be omnipresent is that we are looking for it.

Our experience of perception is that it is a one-way process. Touch your finger to your tongue; does your tongue feel the finger or does the finger feel the tongue? Can you do both at the same time?

Perhaps the higher level of consciousness is not perceivable; perhaps there is a seventh dimension that does the perceiving.

Chapter Eighteen

What if perception isn't just a one-way street? And what if Believing – or Knowing – is the path to seeing. This is not just frou-frou, Marin-speak. Modern science may be on the road to just such a determination.

In this century, those who are in the business of knowing – science is from the Latin *scire* meaning to know – are in the process of turning our perception of reality on its head. Scientists now eschew the very concept of what we think of as solid matter. They say that when you break down stuff like rocks and trees and flesh into atoms and electrons, you wind up with very small particles in vast reaches of empty space.

For most people, this perspective is inconceivable; knock on wood. When the physicists – and these are the mainstream folks in the field – go on to talk about light and photons being both particles and waves, and about probabilities rather than realities, that's when I feel that we seem to be moving away from knowledge. But they begin to reel me in again when they talk about interconnectedness.

The movie *Mindwalk* attempts to make some of these concepts more accessible through a conversation among Liv Ullman (playing a scientist), Sam Waterston (a politician), and John Heard (a poet). Loosely based on Fritjof Capra's book *The Turning Point* and shot at Mont-Saint-Michel, the film illuminates the failure of the *old* mechanistic, Cartesian science that would break everything down into parts, and instead suggests a look at systems theory.

(Sidebar: I did not know what this movie was about when I picked it up off the rack at the video store yesterday. There was an intriguing picture on the box, and it looked neither violent nor stupid. Twelve years earlier, I was contracted to write a proposal for a PBS hour on Capra's book. I was given the book to read, and I was astounded at its scope and the depth – from the standpoints of both new physics and the old politics that were/are governing contemporary society. I wrote up a proposal instead for a four-part series of ninety-minute programs. Unfortunately, the producer, a veteran of the PBS documentary world, hadn't actually read the book himself, and consequently refused to read what I had written. I don't know that he would have understood either the book or the proposal anyway.)

Systems theory is all about interconnectedness. Whether you think of a house of cards or a swimming pool filled with ping pong balls, the idea is the same: everything is connected. More esoterically, as the story goes, when a butterfly flaps its wings over the Yangtze River in Asia, it causes a fluctuation in air currents that winds up producing a storm that will strike the Sacramento Valley in a few days.

Of course there is an interconnectedness – through gravity, atmosphere, sound, and light to name a few of obvious scientific media. Watch the Golden State Warriors when they are on their game; their connectivity can be awesome. Or dancers or lovers. Or just plain ordinary folks in every day interactions.

In his book *The Silent Pulse*, George Leonard recounted a laboratory experiment in which two people were recorded on high-speed film simply speaking with each other. When the film was closely examined, it was discovered that as a person spoke, every separate unit of sound was accompanied by a full series of concomitant body movements that exactly mirrored the duration of the sound.

Is There a Why?

The word "ask", for example, was broken down in this high-speed film into five distinctly separate bits of sounds, and the person saying the word manifested five unique series of body movements for each part of the sound. The entire human system was demonstrating itself in separate, identifiable segments.

But what made the study even more interesting was the fact that the person listening also went through a series of body movements that also exactly paralleled the time frames of the five sounds.

How was this possible? What was the connection between the two people? Did the sound drive the body movements? Do the visual cues reinforce the sound? Where does one person stop and the other start?

Remember a few years ago when a huge fungus, many square miles in size, was discovered in Michigan? It turned out to be a single organism. And more recently, I read that all of the trees in a grove of aspens are interconnected. Are these just odd (if interesting) facts about plant systems, or are they metaphors – or templates – for the all systems? And perhaps for all systems being one system?

Do you resonate with this notion?

If you saw *Interlude* some time back on PBS, the story of Frederic Chopin (Hugh Grant) and George

Sands (Judy Davis), you should remember the scene when he is playing and she is lying on the floor with her head under the piano. She is in a state of reverie with his music. She is resonating to the sounds. Her entire body is experiencing the otic perfection.

When Ella Fitzgerald died, many people celebrated her as a wonderful singer. But it is the nature of our society that most people probably remembered her for the "Is it live or is it Memorex?" television commercials in which she sang a note and shattered a wine glass. There's something about that image that came to mind lately.

When she hit that note, the glass broke apart. There was a splash of shattered pieces, ostensibly random. But actually, the breaks must have taken place where the seams between the glass particles was least strong. But given perfect conditions and the perfect delivery of the perfect sound, every particle should separate from every other.

What if that process is reversed? What if somehow a note could be sounded that would assemble particles together appropriately? Sort of like when the drill sergeant blows his whistle and the troops fall into formation. Or how a television synchronizes those 525 separate horizontal lines (U.S.) into a viewable image.

Or maybe how our bodies work. After all, what keeps all the parts together? Something instructs the molecules to stay in conjunction and alignment; my fingers stay with me and don't affix to someone else when I shake hands with her. If our bodies are what the scientists say, small particles and huge spaces, what is keeping us from flying all apart?

I wouldn't be surprised to learn that what keeps each person together as a physical unit is some kind of unique vibrational pattern. It would also make sense that those *vibes* would extend beyond the skin surface. It would explain how we can *get a feeling* about certain people; how we can know when certain people walk into a room. Is it not plausible that the vibrational pattern that defines itself through voiceprints, polygraphs, and Kurlian photography is also a representation of our mind, of our Self-Personality construct?

Music is a global presence; it exists in some form in every culture. Monks chant. Mediators say *aum*, enunciating all five vowels in the process. As Darwin noted (quoted by Sherlock Holmes), "Before there was language, there was music." We sing together. We raise our voices to the heavens. At least half of the people I see out running and walking are wearing headsets, many of them no doubt listening to music.

People have different tastes in music, but do you

know anyone who doesn't like at least some kind of music?

Music reaches inside of us. It gets us to tap our feet or drum our fingers without thinking. Plants are known to thrive when music is part of the environment. Music is played in offices and stores to induce a positive feeling, of security and abundance.

Or as William Congreve put it three centuries ago, "Music has charms to soothe a savage breast, To soften rocks, or bend a knotted oak."

Hmm.

The same sort of vibrational universality exists with vision. We don't actually see anything, but rather our eyes register the bounce of light particles off objects in our purview. Our eyes register about 25 pictures every second, which are enough recordings to make normal motion appear fluid. When we are presented with a high-speed stream of pictures, as in some 70 frame-per-second films, it can actually disturb our equilibrium.

Research has also determined that different colors generate different emotional responses; some colors incite, while others pacify. Patterns of lines, shapes, and opacities will elicit varied reactions from different people. Different levels of chroma and lumens can induce different behavior. Strobe lights can cause dizziness.

Sound and sight are two dominant forms of inter-connectedness. We are inundated with audio and video, much of it beyond our range of perception. And of what is available to us, we only hear and see a small percentage. Consciously and uncon-sciously, we filter out huge amounts of these sen-sory inputs; otherwise, we would be overwhelmed.

We know about the interconnectedness of sight and sound from our senses. And through our intu-ition we know of a much greater, non-sensory interconnectedness. But we literally cannot imagine the scope and power of this force and our partici-pation in it. At least not yet.

<u>Chapter Nineteen</u>

The other evening, I took to dinner two friends of mine who hadn't yet met each other. I have known Wendy Palmer for fourteen years; she has instructed me in aikido, intuition, and meditation. I met Cathy Adachi only last summer, when I went to her for cranial-sacral therapy for a chronic back problem. After an hour with her, my back felt better than it had in twenty-five years.

I knew nothing about their backgrounds, but wanted to bring them together because they are bright, grounded, and truly fine people. They know a lot about being human, and have given much of themselves to teaching in a productive way. They live healthy, balanced lives, and they contribute significantly to the well-being of others.

The dinner lasted more than three hours, and covered a lot of ground. Much of it sharing of life philosophies based on experience and thought and pain and growth. As I heard their stories, I learned that Wendy had grown up outside of Chicago, and moved to California in the early Seventies. Cathy had spent her childhood in Japan, and didn't come to the United States until she was in her teens. Wendy went to a girls prep school in Maryland; Cathy, it turned out, was enrolled in the same school a year after Wendy graduated.

I think that is a remarkable coincidence, but would it be defined as synchronicity? Certainly their years at the prep school helped to some degree to define who they are today, three decades later, but that definition was not what induced me to bring them together. Nor do I know of any purpose or value for either of them in meeting at this dinner, other than the opportunity to connect with someone of a similarly committed and substantial lifestyle.

It's possible that Wendy and Cathy will never see each other again. It may be that I am the only personal connection that they will ever have. They have played significant roles in my life, expanding my consciousness in critical ways, and deepening my own sense of purpose. Considering the paths that their lives have taken – circumnavigating the globe, learning from teachers on several continents – it seems like something of a stretch to say that it is merely a coincidence that they both came into my life.

Synchronicity, then, is different from coincidence in

that it has the component of meaningfulness. We don't have to know immediately what is that meaning, even if we recognize the synchrony. Sometimes the role we play in the lives of others is not visible to us, but can nevertheless be important.

For much of the past sixteen years, as I was trying to parse my professional life into some form that would generate income, I found that I spent many hours in meetings and in writing proposals, and invested a huge amount of hope in projects that would never come to fruition; some were even absurdly unlikely.

But during the past few years, I became aware that it might be the only purpose of these contacts and ideas that I had invested hope in them. Otherwise, not having anywhere else for my attention to be focused, I might have been unstrung by an over-powering sense of aimlessness.

Here, again, was an example of the internal dialectic: one part of my mind was telling another that I had some viable irons in the fire. Looking back, in some instances, I was unconscionably gullible. I took flyers on my own hopes that challenged my own credulity. But I can't imagine how I would have gotten through if I hadn't thought that I was moving forward. Like a shark that has to keep swimming for water to move through its gills to breathe.

Is There a Why?

Why have I lived my life? If there is a greater scheme of things, what has been my role in it? How have I contributed to the betterment of the species? Have the years to date been preparatory for something to come, including, perhaps, this book? Is it beyond imagination to think that my forty-five years on this planet might (or not) actually have a purpose? Or is it beyond Personalityism to think that some higher consciousness is programming my movements, learning, participation, et cetera?

Until I was in my thirties, I didn't even know the possibility of a Larger Reality even existed. But when I came to understand that there might be *something going on*, I was frustrated beyond comprehension by my not being able to get a cognitive understanding of (1) what It was or even might be, and (2) what could be my use to, of, or in It.

What brings me to writing this book is the deepening realization that there is, in fact, something going on. This realization comes concurrently with the decreasing need to grasp It cognitively. Intuitively, it makes perfect sense.

A wonderful book, one that I've read several times, that provides a friendly framework to appreciating simplicity – that is, unclogging the mind of our societally-installed complexities – is Benjamin Hoff's *The Tao of Pooh*. It is a marvelous read and well as being very informative with the characters of A. A. Milne's *Winnie the Pooh* explaining some of the basic concepts of Taoism. Sort of a metaphor of a metaphor of life.

As simple as are many of the ideas, I got more out of each read. For instance, this quote from Chuang-tse:

A well-frog cannot imagine the ocean, nor can a summer insect conceive of ice. How then can a scholar understand the Tao? He is restricted by his own learning.

Very simple, and obvious, that we are not able to see the Larger Reality because we are restricted by our own learning. But the fact is that replacing what we *know* with new knowledge is very difficult and often upending. The whole scheme of learning is based on assimilating what is already *known* and working from there, so resistance to replacement is not unexpected.

This structure makes sense, sort of, since where else would you start. But inherent in this process is the creation of a foundation of *knowledge* generated by people who are following the same path but earlier. Considering that society – at large, or a particular discipline – rewards those who learn what is taught, we have a system of accumulation rather than of new discovery; adherence, acquiescence, and obeisance rather than true learning.

Growth and change through this configuration can

only, at best, be incremental. And we must presume that the tools of discovery that precede whatever might come along were not as finely developed as the ones we have today. Which means that they likely generated conclusions that are inaccurate, but are still the foundations of subsequent search and determination. This is why science keeps coming up with new understandings that sometimes directly contradict what was *known* before.

(Sidebar: Can't you just picture those three scientists in white lab coats and plastic pocket-protectors standing behind a lectern at a news conference saying, "We used to think but now we know.")

Of course, it's hard to imagine how the process of acquiring knowledge might be done differently. Unless, perhaps, we upset the hierarchical structure, looked at a newborn babe, and waited for it to teach us, taking reverential care of it in the meantime. This would certainly make more sense, given the presumption of the Spirit incarnating, but it certainly wouldn't augur well for those benefitting from the current social structure.

So far, we haven't tried this, which means that the planet is populated by five billion *grown-ups* who have spent years adapting to the local social regulations and pushing out of their mind whatever knowledge they came into this life with. The awareness of a Larger Reality requires an unlearning of the social overlay which has been drilled into us until we are as practiced at performing our individual role in every day life as Steph Curry is at making a three-pointer.

We not only need some sort of instigation to peel back the layers of the learned onion – an instigation that will push us past the life-threatening alarms and hidden traps that our Personality has been built in to protect us from our true Self – but we need to know that there in fact exists a route back to our source, and some way to find it.

I don't think we all get that prodding, or that those who do take the necessary steps. For some, it is simply too painful. For some, it is not yet time. But when you look at it not in the context of individuals taking this journey, but of a systemic change of which certain individuals are the first voyagers, then it begins to make some sense.

Its like we are individual trees in that aspen grove, or hunks of that massive Michigan mushroom. We have our roles in massing and catalyzing. We are the hundredth monkey.

That that monkey didn't think about the social implications of washing off his sweet potato, or even from where came the thought to do so, is our conundrum and our cause.

Chapter Twenty

The process of unlearning is complicated by the fact that not only was most of the structural foundation of what we *know* established in us as fact decades earlier, usually by the middle of our first year in school, but that it was interwoven into our learned consciousness in a skein that was both intellectual and emotional. And was rooted in our very survival.

People who have been raised in a dominating religion, or in some other system that relies heavily on fear and coercion, have a particularly tough time of unlearning. They have incorporated an intellectual, life-long survival thesis on top of the basic reward-punishment mechanism. Rooting out Catholic guilt indoctrination, for example, is probably as difficult as eliminating vengeance from the heart of a young Palestinian man.

This is why those who are searching for deeper meaning in their lives usually have to bump into new wisdom more than once, and thus why we so often will find ourselves "Aha-ing" at something that we have seen, heard, and/or read before, perhaps many times or many years earlier. The layering process of learning requires a complex disassembling of long-ago generated integral internal mechanisms. Sometimes we have to be hit over the head with the *obvious* before we are able to see something, and that's usually when the real work begins.

The good news, however, is that seeing the anachronism – the calcified presumption – is the key to enlightenment. You can choose not to follow up, but at least you've seen the truth. Reaching that point of choice is where the new life begins.

*   *   *   *   *

No one can achieve awareness for you. You can't buy awareness. No amount of workshops, books, or drugs will induce it. But you can meet people who will say or show you things that you will be able to connect to your own experiences that may help to expand your consciousness. Often, you will find that you have known something, but needed a new context in which to fit it.

But you also don't have to believe in anything. You can simply come to know it. More accurately, you come to find that you already knew.

Is There a Why?

*   *   *   *   *

When I woke up on the morning after Christmas 1985, I remembered vividly a curious dream. I was standing with a group of people and I was trying to strangle someone with my bare hands. It wasn't a violent scene; on the contrary, it was quite calm. I had my hands around his throat and I was trying to choke him to death. But I couldn't. He just stood there, as did the others, watching, patient, waiting for me to realize that I couldn't strangle him.

The him was a man named Harry. And Harry was my Self. I had dreamt about Harry before and have since a few times, and recognized him as embodying the better aspects of my person; without the Personalityism that I associate with Tony. How clear am I on this relationship? When I was writing the last paragraph, I first typed "my hands around my throat." (I thought of leaving it that way, but it seemed less confusing to say it this way.)

What is curious to me is that while I have reprised the memory of that dream a number of times over the years, and have had in my mind this framework of Self and Personality, it wasn't until this week that I saw the connection between the dream image and the philosophical construct outlined in these pages of the Personality trying to choke off the Self.

Is There a Why?

This story is significant to me in two ways; for its content, and for the fact that it kept reprising in my consciousness until it found its place. (It also underscores the value of contemplating the messages in our dreams. As bizarre as some images may be, they must have some purpose; otherwise, why would we remember them? Why would these images transit from the non-conscious to the conscious mind?)

Why does awareness take so long? Why isn't the obvious obvious? Because learning, and unlearning, is not a linear process; thoughts are less lines than they are webs. And this metaphor is worth another comment: the network of ideas and beliefs that comprise our picture of who we are is like a spider's web in that it must be continually maintained or it falls apart.

When, in the process of enlightenment and increasing awareness, we start wondering about reality, we necessarily turn our attention away and stop feeding the familiar scenario. We can't invest in both the old and the new. And the more we shift perceptions from autonomic endorsement of the social reality to our own enlightened view, the more we see holes in the old picture.

Usually when we discover tears in our perception of the social fabric, it is with the recognition that we've known that they were there all along, but we didn't want to see them. After all, if you say to yourself that the emperor is naked, then you ultimately have to alter – and sometimes sever – your ties with all of those friends, colleagues, neighbors, and family who are quite adamant about his wardrobe, and particularly vocal about to the details.

If we are on course for a transformation on the scale that is suggested and warranted by events, the hundredth monkey will not be an individual but a sizable group of people. That's one of the unique aspects of this change; it is a collective instigation. Tina Turner wailed, "We don't need another hero." In fact, we are to be the Heroes of our own time.

What if two percent of the population were such early adapters, pioneering a shift? What would look different if there were six million (neo-) enlightened people in this country? Might they already be here and already on the road to higher consciousness, but just not coalesced? What might unify them?

An old friend said he believed that ten thousand leaders were born out of the anti-war movement in the 70s. There were probably as many leaders born out of the civil rights and women's liberation movements. Toss in the New Age, right livelihood entrepreneurs, and now the Internet and social media, and you have to think that we could be approaching critical mass. And probably none too soon.

I believe that this final, pre-consciousness phase may have been triggered by the detonation of the first atomic bombs. In a very real sense, the application of physics to design, produce, and explode the power-of-the-atom weapon on fellow human beings signaled our ability – and apparent crypto-willingness – to annihilate ourselves.

It was the ultimate act of the left lobe, the masculine power mind, the contra-intuitive. Like the strange vacuum creature in *Yellow Submarine* that sucked up everything until it sucked itself up and ended existence.

Dropping those bombs on Japan marked a turning point; from that pinnacle of intellectual pointlessness, we made a shift. And from the proverbial loins of that era came the girls who would be the army behind the women's liberation movement; the movement to incorporate feminine values like intuition into the social consciousness. And it birthed the boys who would say that war was no longer a viable option.

These detonations were the bottom of the pendulum swing. They simultaneously marked the nadir of the old order and the beginning of the new. Einstein wasn't so optimistic in 1946:

Is There a Why?

The unleashed power of the atom has changed everything save our modes of thinking and we thus drift toward unparalleled catastrophe.

But perhaps it is that because he, too, was of the old order he mis-read the signs and that we will transform catastrophe into a skip up the evolutionary ladder. Maybe the people born after August 1945 were cellularly different. It could be that they were infused with a new awareness, a spiritual imperative that would turn us away from a mechanistic totalitarianism that could only lead to extinction, and move us instead to find purpose in life.

Maybe the global acceleration of totalitarianism since the election of Donald Trump will push us, finally cause a polar shift from the political right to the moral right.

Chapter Twenty-One

What would induce six million people to take a flyer on a higher level of consciousness? In part, perhaps, it might be the conclusion that the social structure of which they have been a part will no longer be sustaining. And looking around today, there is plenty of evidence to support that premise.

Power – money and guns – are in the hands of people whose personal interests are in conflict with those of society's future. Management of our institutions has devolved from the innovators and designers to the bureaucrats and administrators. Our institutions themselves are disintegrating, our leaders lack vision, and apathy, despair and distrust are rising like a toxic cloud from the decay of our own social organism.

Hardly good news for those who miss the world of *Ozzie and Harriet* – the promise of the post-war era. The plan was to settle down after World War Two into a peace that was defined as the *Life of Riley*:

you're born, you die, and you work at the same job all your life until you can retire, and pay off the mortgage on your house. Sounds familiar. Throw in church, good manners, and pride in America and you have the somnolent package that Beaver and Wally looked forward to. It was the middle of the Twentieth Century, and we had arrived.

The only problem was that while this picture might be enough for the politicians and the bankers, status quo wouldn't survive the reality check of evolution. Even if we had been able to keep the population down, and to spread our idea of comfort to the rest of the world, the natural progression to expanded consciousness – the realization of the potential of the human being – could not be squelched. It had been going on for a million years, and it was not going to be stopped by a second car in the Cunningham's garage.

The impulsion was always in the works. The same cerebral scheme that invented trains and boats and planes, and the atom bomb, was seeking realization of its higher capacity. It could not operate in a stultifying environment. It needed chaos, a stirring of the pot, to discover new combinations to allow and encourage the creative process.

In our mechanistic-capitalist society, with spirituality marginalized to a bloodless Sunday morning ritual, and with art co-opted into an accessory of the rich, there was little in the system to instigate significant growth and change. In retrospect, we can look back at the beatniks of the Fifties and then the hippies of the Sixties as fomenters, but if there was a single moment that signaled an end to the dream, it was probably the assassination of John Kennedy. As the great American protest singer Phil Ochs put it, Kennedy was *A man so filled with life, even Death was caught off guard.*

Whether or not you think the killer was Lee Harvey Oswald, the larger truth was told by Mick Jagger when he sang, "I shouted out who killed those Kennedy's, when after all it was you and me." He was referring to society, of course, but a broader perspective would suggest the greater context of the Larger Reality.

If you accept the systems theory and recognize that the individual is part of the whole, then Kennedy's death was more than the death of one man. As Donne said, and as is evidenced by the fact that every American over the age of 65 can tell you where they were when they heard the news from Dallas. Kennedy's assassination represented, at least in the national psyche, more than the death of a man or even the killing of a president. It was the death of our societal innocence. And regardless of what the revisionists have to say about Kennedy's role in the Bay of Pigs or Vietnam or Marilyn Monroe, he was arguably the last American hero; certainly the last president we liked.

As much as we would mourn him, the death of this one individual founted the Civil Rights Act of 1964, and probably also unleashed the Sixties counter-cultural assaults on racism, gender bias, and war. Since then, our presidents have been corrupt or ineffectual or both; and what does that say about the world's premiere democracy? Perhaps that it is not working.

The Gnostic belief has it that there are two worlds: the horizontal which is the every-day, temporal world of working, eating, and the general conduct of what most of us call life; and the vertical which is a trans-temporal (multi-lifetime) ascension of a spiritual ladder from lower to higher consciousness.

Who's to say that there isn't some merit to this view? Indeed, most of the people on the planet think that there's more to life than life. Which certainly makes sense, since the lives that the vast majority of them are living don't seem worth much in themselves. Which suggests the potential for a *successful* transformation, once the stampeding herd is turned away from its path toward the cliff.

Paul Ehrlich noted that if you put a frog in a pan of boiling water, the frog will jump out. But if you put the frog in a pan of water and start to heat it, the frog will cook. I think most of us haven't cognitized the fact that the temperature has been rising for the past seventy years; although on a visceral level, the discomfort has become quite palpable.

We are discovering that we have been programmed to think things that (1) aren't in our own best interests, and (2) don't make sense when held up to the light. What's good for General Motors, it turns out is not good for America. Nor is bigger always better. And it's not true that the person who dies with the most toys wins. We have the highest per capita prison population and by far the largest military budget and yet we feel less safe. We spend billions of dollars on political campaigns, but fewer people vote.

Surely the contradictions will catch up with us. More and more people will realize that *it's not working*; that what was once a viable social structure isn't coping and isn't fixable. But it is replaceable. Once we recognize that the incremental change has fallen too far behind to catch up, that we need to start afresh, then we can reformulate our definitions of who and what we are, and from there, design a social organization that incorporates an honest reality.

Those who adhere to and profit from the current view are obviously not going to jump on this bandwagon. The degree of their resistance will determine how smoothly a transition might be made; how much collateral damage will be incurred.

If we are in a process that enables them to relax their grip enough so that their power can dissipate, then we will make the changes faster and with less carnage. It will not, however, be because a god appears, or by means of a magic potion. It will necessarily be wrenching and traumatic, incomprehensibly so, because that's what death and chaos and birth are about.

At this level of change, of ending social organization as we know it, of re-creating civilization based on individuals contributing their best Self(s) to the commonweal instead of performing according to anachronistic lights; when a whole planetful of our species needs to shift direction away from thousands of years of history, it's going to get unseemly in many respects. This is necessarily so because we are in a period of deepening chaos that is generating the compost out of our past to fertilize our future.

Those who lack the awareness to understand this transformation, those who see a threat to their own well-being, will fight to preserve what they have. And they will say that they are doing so for the good of us all. They will accuse the pioneers of doing the devil's work. Viz, the Islamic movement abroad, and the religious right in this country.

Of course there is going to be this fear in response to change, but there is also this clarifying point: there really is no such thing as Evil. As atrocious as we might justly find certain behavior, it is always and only the act of an individual, or of individuals operating under a group dynamic. The notion of a Satanic force was created to condemn and ostracize those who wouldn't submit to the social order. And the foundation tenet of this clarified truth is located in the very Christian suggestion to love the sinner and hate the sin.

The Spirit grows in one direction, toward fulfillment. It rises like a bubble through water. It is not about individuals but process, and people are part of that process. Incarnated in myriad Self(s), the Spirit has flowed through the minds of billions of Personalties and the circumstances of millennia to reach where we are today...and to move us on to where we are going. There is nothing perverse in the Self, but it would be ridiculous not to understand that channeled through a Personality that has been molested and maligned beyond reason, some pretty atrocious behavior can be expected. That is the result of society, not the Spirit.

In this time of transformation, as our moorings are cut, as the world seems to spin faster, as our lives seem to lose their meaning and we our control of them, we need to avoid the societalized tendency to attack that which we don't understand or that conflicts with what we think is the only way. We must also check our *instincts* to look outside of ourselves for stability or even understanding. And we must also allow that some people, in desperation and ignorance, may look and, temporarily at least, find a respite from the turmoil in fundamentalism, the alt-right, or living off the grid..

But no longer will it work to seek clarity from those who say they are listening to god. Not when we can listen to god ourselves, our Self.

Epilogue

In February of 1982, I had gone home to Massachu-setts to attend my sister's wedding. The day after the festivities were over and everyone had left, I spent the day with my mother. That evening, we were sitting at the kitchen table talking. I had been on the West Coast for fifteen months at that point, had ended a four-month marriage, didn't have a job, and was talking of ideas about a Larger Reality that didn't sit well in the house of the life that I had left. Also, they were new ideas to me, and I was not adept at explaining them.

At one point, out of frustration with her unwilling-ness to hear me, I asked my mother,

"Do you love me?"

"Yes," she said.

"As your son?" I clarified.

"Yes."

"As a person?" I asked.

Is There a Why?

"I don't know you."

"Do you want to?"

That flustered her. Had I been more aware or sensitive, I would have realized that to do so – to know the ideas I was trying to explain – would have shaken her to her roots, and jeopardized her relationship with my father; which was not something I would have wished. As I felt it then, the basic tenet of my upbringing had been an unbridled search for (intellectual) truth, and here she was going back on that commitment. I felt that I had been cut loose.

In a matter of moments, my pain and fury exploded out at her as it never had before. Verbally; we were not a physical family. I was outraged, and showed it, saying something like "If I sat in the middle of this fucking floor and levitated, then would you listen to me?" We didn't use words like that in our house, but it was more the sentiments and where the conversation was headed that prompted her response. She ordered me out of the house.

I went upstairs to pack, my anger quickly giving way to a deep sense of loss and sadness. She came up a few moments later and told me that she didn't want me to go this way. We hugged each other and meant it. The schism was still there, but it was only intellectual; and that wasn't enough, even in our family, to hold onto the anger. I was leaving for California the next day anyway, and neither of us, with our decades of love and respect would have wanted our differences to cause an indelible rift, especially when we would be three thousand miles apart.

*   *   *   *   *

Eight months later, I sat on the edge of my mother's hospital bed. The Hodgkin's disease which had ravaged her immune system for more than a decade was playing out its final act. She had gotten food poisoning on a trip to Paris the week before. My sister had managed to get her back to the States, but my mother had decided she couldn't go through another course of chemotherapy.

For a week, she had been on enough morphine to keep away the pain. And asleep. The family had been maintaining the vigil of the inevitable, waiting for her body to acquiesce. On the Monday night before the Saturday morning that she died, she hadn't been lucid for days. I was getting ready to say goodnight to her sleeping form when suddenly, she opened her eyes and looked at me as brightly as if she had never been sick a day in her life.

"What time is it?" she asked me, smiling warmly.

I twisted my head around to look at the clock on the opposite wall and turned back to find her eyes on me. "It's ten-oh-six," I told her.

"You're right," she affirmed. And then she closed her eyes. They were the last words she spoke.

*   *   *   *   *

There is a Larger Reality. It is evolving through us, as we evolve in our individual lives. Its purpose seems to be to expand our consciousness, our awareness of a broader reality, and it has been doing this at least since the beginning of recorded history. Well, probably from the beginning of time.

It is evident in the world's religions, in our cultures and our myths, and in our every day lives.

Though not quite visible – though certainly more perceptible to those who presume and seek, with every passing moment – this Larger Reality is moving inexorably closer to realization, through individuals, on a global scale.

The more we look into it, toward our Self(s), the more evidence we find of the true Nature of our existence, and the mutuality of evolution and god. The more we go inside, the more we see and align with this greater truth.

The discord in our lives is a consequence of our being out of alignment with the Larger Reality; the dissonance being the result of our attempt to align with the temporal reality.

The negativity we experience is our guidance system, warning us when we are about to bump into the sides of the proverbial tunnel that leads to the light. The negativity is not punitive. It provides us with the opportunity to fine-tune the direction and conduct of our journey.

The myriad Self(s) who share our planet are all each sourced of the Spirit, each of us a part of a systemic creation seeking a vibrational harmony.

When enough of us as individuals find our Self(s) trued in alignment, we will reach critical mass and join in transcendence to the next level.

About the Author

Tony Seton is a journalist, writer, publisher, public speaker, business/political consultant, and communications specialist. As a broadcast journalist for ABC TV, he covered Watergate, six elections, and five space shots, produced Barbara Walters' news interviews, and won national awards for his business/economics coverage.

Later, he wrote and produced two award-winning public television documentaries. He has conducted over 2,600 interviews, and is the author of more than 2,300 essays.

Through Seton Publishing, he has edited and published 35 of his own books, and 33 for clients. He has also written several screenplays.

As a political consultant, his clients have included Nancy Pelosi, Tom Campbell, the American Nurses Association, and a plethora of local candidates.

He has taught journalism and writing, provided media training, and produced websites.

Tony is also a private pilot and a photographer.

SETON
PUBLISHING

www.ingramcontent.com/pod-product-compliance
Lightning Source LLC
Chambersburg PA
CBHW061431040426
42450CB00007B/1005